The publication of this book has been made possible by support received from

Ahujasons Shawl Wale (P) Ltd
Bhulabhai & Dhirajlal Desai Memorial Trust
Arvind Limited
Bakeri Engineering & Infrastructure Ltd

General Editor
PRATAPADITYA PAL

Senior Executive Editor
SAVITA CHANDIRAMANI
Senior Editorial Executive
ARNAVAZ K. BHANSALI
Editorial Executive
RAHUL D'SOUZA

Text Editor
RIVKA ISRAEL

Designer
NAJU HIRANI
Senior Production Executive
GAUTAM V. JADHAV

Vol. 63 No. 2
December 2011
Price: ₹ 2800.00 / US$ 68.00
ISBN: 978-81-921106-0-8
Library of Congress Catalog Card Number: 2011-312022

Marg is a registered trademark of The Marg Foundation
© The Marg Foundation, 2011
All rights reserved

No part of this publication may be reproduced, stored, adapted, or transmitted, in any form or by any means, electronic, mechanical, photocopying, recording, or otherwise, or translated in any language or performed or communicated to the public in any manner whatsoever, or any cinematographic film or sound recording made therefrom without the prior written permission of the copyright holders.
This edition may be exported from India only by the publishers, The Marg Foundation, and by their authorized distributors and this constitutes a condition of its initial sale and its subsequent sales.
Published by Radhika Sabavala for The Marg Foundation at Army & Navy Building (3rd Floor), 148, M.G. Road, Mumbai 400 001, India.
Printed at Spenta Multimedia, Mumbai and
Processed at The Marg Foundation, Mumbai.

Captions to preliminary pages:
Page 1: View of Sangath foyer. Photograph courtesy Sangath.
Pages 2–3: see page 136.
Pages 4–5: Blockprinted fabrics drying on the riverbed: an iconic image of the Sabarmati till recently. Photograph © Dinodia Images.
Pages 6–7: see page 92.

Marg's quarterly publications receive support from the Sir Dorabji Tata Trust – Endowment Fund

Contents

8	Map
9	Introduction
20	Architectural Traditions of the Evolving City *R.J. Vasavada*
34	Ahmedabad as a Centre of Painting *Shridhar Andhare*
50	Arabic-Persian Scholarship: Medieval Manuscripts at the Hazrat Pir Muhammad Shah Dargah Sharif Library *Mohaiuddin Bombaywala*
64	Incubating Indian Modernism *Himanshu Burte*
80	An Awakening of Modern Art *Sharmila Sagara*
94	Food is Serious Business *Sheela Bhatt*
106	The Legend of Sabarmati's Hand-Blockprinted Textiles *Aditi Ranjan*
124	Paper, *Chopda*s, Kites: Crafting Hindu-Muslim Symbiosis *Suchitra Balasubrahmanyan*
140	Ahmedabad 600: Readings from the Palimpsest *Yatin Pandya*
154	Index
156	Contributors

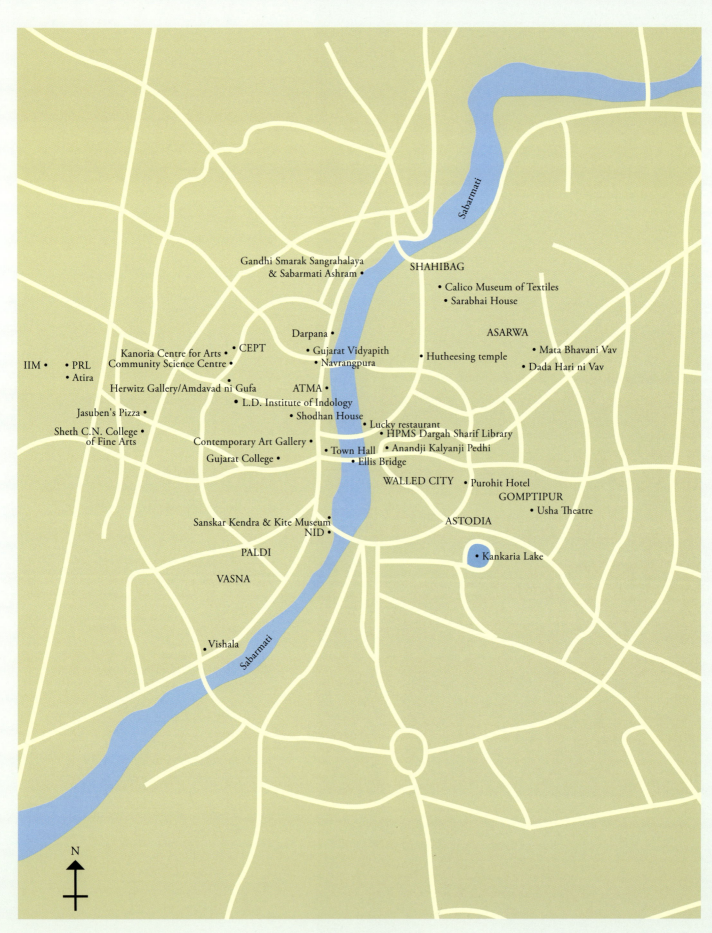

This map has been adapted by Dylan Drego from material provided by Jigna Desai.

Introduction

Suchitra Balasubrahmanyan and Sharmila Sagara

This volume presents portraits of one of India's most prosperous cities on the occasion of the 600th anniversary of its foundation. Established in 1411 by Sultan Ahmed Shah and named after him, Ahmedabad was a magnificent "City of Beauties" from the early years after its inception. Abul Fazl called Ahmedabad "a noble city in a high state of prosperity" and its riches later drew the Marathas and the British to it. And it has continued to prosper, unlike its contemporaries, which today are either in ruins or insignificant towns with none of their former glory. This steady expansion and growth has been possible because the city and its citizens have continuously transformed to respond to the changing social, political, and economic challenges that each passing century has posed. In the process it has acquired blemishes too. For the disgusted Mughal emperor Jahangir it was *gardabad* (dusty city), *bimaristan* (land of the ill), and *jahannamabad* (hellish city). Dalpatram, the eminent Gujarati poet of the 19th century, drew attention to the city's filth, while Mahatma Gandhi despaired of its excessive *vaishyavritti*, the tendency of Ahmedabadis to see all aspects of life in terms of profit and loss. Yet, the city's ever-expanding urban boundaries are still organically linked to its medieval core with the modern and the traditional faces influencing and moulding each other. Which is why this volume takes the form of portraits, in the plural, as no one view of Ahmedabad can do justice to the city's multifaceted complexity.

The City's Birth and Growth
The early years of the 15th century were the twilight years of the Delhi Sultanate when provincial leaders found the opportunity to break free of the waning power and authority of Delhi and established independent sultanates in different parts of the subcontinent. One such noble was Zafar Khan who established the independent Gujarat Sultanate in 1407, assuming the title Muzaffar Shah I. It was during the reign of his grandson Ahmed Shah that the Gujarat Sultanate was consolidated and came into its own. The decisive moment was when Ahmed Shah laid the foundation of a new capital on the banks of the Sabarmati river in 1411, asserting and underlining his authority by ending the association with Patan which had been the capital of Gujarat since the 10th century.

The Sultanate period lasted about 200 years during which Ahmedabad became a prosperous trading and craft-manufacturing centre. Under successive sultans, particularly Mahmud Begada and Muzaffar Shah II, Ahmedabad's architecture, art, crafts, and textiles flowered. The city exerted a centripetal force, drawing skill and scholarship from all over the subcontinent and the larger pan-Islamic community of West Asia. Simultaneously, the centrifugal force of Indian Ocean trade networks took Ahmedabadis as far east as Malacca and west to Africa. In 1573, after a battle on the banks of the Sabarmati, Akbar took over Ahmedabad and annexed Gujarat to the Mughal empire. Gujarat was prized not only for its wealth and manufactures but also because its ports, particularly Cambay (Khambat) lying 70 kilometres south of Ahmedabad, were the gateways to Mecca. For European traders, Cambay was the gateway to India and it was in the Mughal period that Ahmedabad had its first encounter with Dutch and English traders who established factories in the city to deal in textiles, indigo, saltpetre, and paper. However, though Ahmedabad was visited by Europeans much before other major Indian cities, there was no substantive cultural impact.

As Mughal power waned, there began in the early 18th century a tumultuous period of political uncertainty and economic instability during which the Marathas pillaged Gujarat's cities. Ahmedabad escaped plunder through the determined action of its most wealthy trader Kushalchand (he had earlier received the title of Nagarsheth, head of the city, from the Mughal emperor in the early 18th century), who personally paid off the Maratha hordes. Kushalchand earned the everlasting gratitude of his fellow Ahmedabadis who pledged to pay a percentage of their profits to his family in perpetuity. The city however

1 (previous page)
A rainy day in 1937, by Pranlal Patel.

Contents

8   Map

9   Introduction

20   Architectural Traditions of the Evolving City
R.J. Vasavada

34   Ahmedabad as a Centre of Painting
Shridhar Andhare

50   Arabic-Persian Scholarship: Medieval Manuscripts at the Hazrat Pir Muhammad Shah Dargah Sharif Library
Mohaiuddin Bombaywala

64   Incubating Indian Modernism
Himanshu Burte

80   An Awakening of Modern Art
Sharmila Sagara

94   Food is Serious Business
Sheela Bhatt

106   The Legend of Sabarmati's Hand-Blockprinted Textiles
Aditi Ranjan

124   Paper, *Chopda*s, Kites: Crafting Hindu-Muslim Symbiosis
Suchitra Balasubrahmanyan

140   Ahmedabad 600: Readings from the Palimpsest
Yatin Pandya

154   Index

156   Contributors

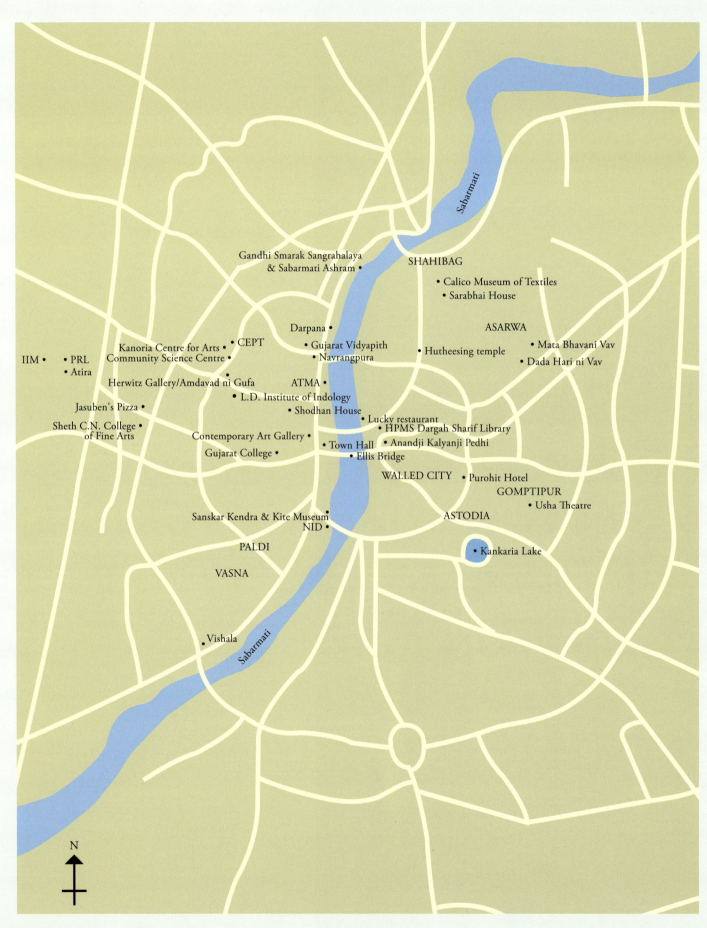

This map has been adapted by Dylan Drego from material provided by Jigna Desai.

came under joint Peshwa and Gaekwad control and this period of political fluidity and anarchy lasted about a century till the English militia laid siege to Ahmedabad and took it over in 1819.

A tenuous English rule was established where the mercantile elite of the city partnered with English administrators to usher in a cultural transformation in the urban landscape of Ahmedabad. The crumbling city walls were repaired, modern education was introduced for boys and girls, piped water and sewage systems were installed, and a railway line connected the city with Bombay. With English assistance, Ranchhodlal Chhotalal established a highly successful textile industry. Printing technology brought newspapers and books to the newly literate, and the Gujarat Vernacular Society was established by Dalpatram and the English judge A.K. Forbes to foster literature and poetry in the Gujarati language.

By the late 19th century Ahmedabadis began to chafe under British rule and a nascent swadeshi movement for greater economic independence gained ground in the 1870s. With the coming of Gandhi in 1915 and the establishment of his ashram and later his university Gujarat Vidyapith in 1920, this assertion was soon transformed into a movement for political autonomy and Ahmedabad became an active centre of the struggle for freedom from colonial rule. Gandhi's institution Puratatva Mandir, which conducted research in ancient Indian culture and languages, coupled with Tagore's visits during this period, ushered in a new phase of intellectual activity in the city. Independence in 1947 was followed by statehood for Gujarat in 1960 and though Gandhinagar was the designated capital, Ahmedabad remained the de facto centre of political and economic power.

Viewing the City
There are many ways in which to draw a portrait of a city such as Ahmedabad. The first is, of course, the historical portrait and there are three significant works in this genre – the 18th-century Persian history *Mirat-i-Ahmadi* by Ali Muhammad Khan, the mid-19th-century Gujarati account *Amdavadno Itihas* by Maganlal Vakhatchand, and the early-20th-century Gujarati chronicle *Gujaratnu Patnagar – Amdavad* by Ratnamanirao Jote. All three start with the foundation of the city, bringing the story up to each author's times. A new genre evolved in the colonial period, that of illustrated accounts of architecture. These were sumptuous publications about the city's monuments brought alive by photography and printing, the two technologies introduced in the late 19th century, prompted by the imperial appetite for the documentation and preservation of "native" arts and architecture. The earliest of these were Theodore Hope and James Fergusson's *Architecture at Ahmedabad, the Capital of Goozerat* (1866), and Jas Burgess's *The Muhammadan Architecture of Ahmadabad* (1900). More recently, George Michell and Snehal Shah's *Ahmadabad* (1988) and Yatin Pandya and Trupti Rawal's *The Ahmedabad Chronicle: Imprints of a Millennium* (2002) have presented architectural aspects of the city. In the 1960s, the focus turned to urban and social histories which analysed the cultural processes which shaped the city, economic forces which propelled these processes, and the underlying political pushes and pulls. Significant among these were Kenneth Gillion's *Ahmedabad: A Study in Indian Urban History* (1968), Makrand Mehta's *The Ahmedabad Cotton Textile Industry: Genesis and Growth* (1982), Achyut Yagnik and Suchitra Sheth's *Ahmedabad: From Royal City to Megacity* (2011), and Howard Spodek's *Ahmedabad: Shock City of Twentieth-Century India* (2011).

The present volume tries to bring together strands from these three ways of looking at Ahmedabad to propose a fourth – a multifaceted, multivocal view which attempts to capture the city in all its cultural complexity. Following this approach, the arts and architecture are viewed not in themselves but against the backdrop of the city elite's patronage structures; the food and craft cultures are appreciated in the light of Ahmedabad's entrepreneurial spirit and early encounters with globalization, as well as in the context of the seemingly paradoxical synthesis and symbiosis between the city's many communities which are sometimes unable to live in peace with each other.

Portraits of a City

In the first essay, architect and historian R.J. Vasavada explores Jain traditions in architecture and demonstrates how these features form the foundation over which the Islamic vocabulary and building techniques were overlaid to result in Ahmedabad's unique pols, mosques, stepwells, and havelis. As the building material changed from wood to stone to modern materials, elements from the earlier forms persist to find a place in subsequent building forms, albeit with changes and transformations (figure 2).

Following this essay on architectural synthesis, is art historian Shridhar Andhare's essay on Ahmedabad as a centre of painting, with a focus on Jain manuscripts and cloth paintings (figure 3). While Jain miniatures had their own style, forms, and symbolism, they absorbed Mughal influences and expressions. Shaped by their religious character and bound by the constraints posed by ritual requirements, Jain paintings flourished through the patronage of Ahmedabad's wealthy Jain merchants and traders who supported this art to gain spiritual merit.

The next chapter presents a fascinating description of Ahmedabad as a pre-eminent centre for Arabic and Persian scholarship in the 15th and 16th centuries. This story is told by Mohaiuddin Bombaywala, a former professor of Urdu at Gujarat Vidyapith who is also the director of the Hazrat Pir Muhammad Shah Dargah Sharif Library. Through the manuscript collection of this library (figure 4) he throws light on the knowledge traditions of medieval Ahmedabad. The essay points to the madrasas and libraries established in the city, the scholars and saints who taught and wrote there. Clearly, none of this would have been possible without scribes, calligraphers, bookbinders, and most importantly papermakers. Arabic-Persian scholarship waned after the arrival of the British and this important side of Ahmedabad is all but forgotten.

2
Gate under a house leading to a cluster of inner houses.
Photograph: R.J. Vasavada, 2011.

3
Stylized depiction of *tirtha*s (sacred sites) from a *vividha-tirtha-pata*, painted on cloth at Ahmedabad in 1641. Collection of Anandji Kalyanji Pedhi, Ahmedabad. Photograph: Shridhar Andhare.

The first three essays focus on the period before the British took control and set in motion an intense churning in the cultural life of the city. The cityscape changed as the walls were rebuilt and textile mills joined the minarets to transform the skyline. Unfortunately, the photographs in the volumes by Hope, Fergusson, and Burgess focus only on the city's medieval architecture and do not give us a glimpse of the modernizing city. And unlike Bombay, Calcutta, and Madras, there are fewer extant buildings in this city which show a British influence. Distinct Gothic features are seen in a few mid-19th-century buildings such as Gujarat College and the Irish Presbyterian Mission school, church, and seminary near Ellis Bridge.

However, we do have rich word-pictures of mid-19th-century changes in Maganlal Vakhatchand's descriptions in *Amdavadno Itihas*. He describes the city's growing prosperity, the men wearing finer fabrics and turbans trimmed with gold and silver, and new houses being built to English designs. This is corroborated by the first essay in this volume which concludes by pointing to the emergence of an imitative Western "bungalow" style adopted by the modern entrepreneurial class which emerged during the late 19th century and the decades before Independence.

The next two essays take up the narrative in the post-Independence period, at the point when Gujarat becomes a state and new forces begin to shape the urban landscape. Himanshu Burte, architectural historian and critic, explores the fascinating saga of how modernism in architecture was incubated in Ahmedabad as the city chose to take the modernist path in creating new institutions of learning and research (figure 5). Tracing the influence of French architect Le Corbusier, the American Louis Kahn, and other local and national architects who were trained in the modernist paradigm, Burte shows the

4
A rare copy of *Majmul Bahrain*, a Persian translation of the Upanishads by Dara Shikoh, c. 16th century. Collection of the Hazrat Pir Muhammad Shah Dargah Sharif Library. Photograph: Kunal Panchal.

lasting impact of these influences, and of the schools of design and architecture that were established here in the 1960s, not only on the city's built environment but on the urban fabric of the rest of the country.

Artist and writer Sharmila Sagara's essay follows Burte's to tell the story of Ahmedabad's art awakening with the introduction of modernism in painting and sculpture in the same period. The early decades of the 20th century saw the development of art that was deeply influenced by the Sir J.J. School of Art in Bombay. Young artists from Gujarat's cities trained here and many came to Ahmedabad where rich millowners offered them patronage and support. Gandhi soon attracted several of them, like Ravishankar Raval and Kanu Desai, and their work acquired a nationalistic character and content. Breaking away from both the semi-classical visual style and the nationalistic approach, Raval's student Chhaganlal Jadav turned to a modernist visual language of exploring abstraction (figure 6). The generation after his, with artists like Piraji Sagara and Jeram Patel, experimented with new materials and forms.

Both Burte and Sagara point to the key role played by the city's textile-millowning families in the 1960s and '70s. The entrepreneurial spirit that they brought to their business was also directed towards the cultural arena, setting in motion a veritable cultural churning. New educational institutions were set up – the National Institute of Design, Indian Institute of Management, Centre for Environment Planning and Technology; India's space programme established a centre here where experiments in community television were conducted. Vikram Sarabhai, scion of one of the leading textile-millowning families, established the Community Science Centre, the first of its kind in the world, to bring science to the public. Interestingly, in the early 1970s a specimen of moon rock brought by the Apollo 11 mission was put on public display at the Physical Research Laboratory (established in Ahmedabad in 1947), accompanied by a lecture by Arthur C. Clarke on the subject.

Experiments in dance were initiated by Bharatanatyam expert Mrinalini Sarabhai and by Kathak exponent Kumudini Lakhia, and their schools, Darpana and Kadamb, became nationally renowned. Significantly, both women married into prominent millowning families. Classical music maestros such as Faiyyaz Khan, Omkarnath Thakur, and Begum Akhtar, to name a few, were regular performers and this legacy continues with the annual Saptak Music Festival which still draws renowned musicians every winter to Ahmedabad. The city had the opportunity to experience experimental Western music and modern dance when John Cage and Merce Cunningham performed at the Town Hall in 1964.

The 1960s and '70s were also the decades when literature and poetry were vibrant in the city. The oldest of Ahmedabad's eminent poets was Akho, an important Bhakti poet of the 16th century; in the 19th century Dalpatram and his son Nanalal were renowned. Sundaram and Umashankar Joshi dominated Gujarati prose and poetry in the 20th century and their younger contemporaries were Niranjan Bhagat, Sheikhadam Abuwala, and Adil Mansuri. In the 1980s, Ahmedabad also became the nerve centre for Dalit literature in Gujarati. The city's artists, poets, and writers nourished each other, and Havmor restaurant became their nightly haunt. This restaurant was also the hub of the city's other great passion, food.

Journalist Sheela Bhatt, for many years a resident of the city, explores Ahmedabad as a place where conspicuous consumption is quite literal and where food is serious business. The entrepreneurial spirit finds expression here too, as feasting on both local Gujarati

5
Manav Sadhna Kendra. Architect Yatin Pandya. Photograph: Himanshu Burte.

6
"Untitled", by Chhaganlal Jadav. Oil on canvas. Collection: Chhaganlal Jadav Trust.

7
View of Manek Chowk at night with a stall selling Cadbury Pizza, Pineapple Sandwich and Pineapple Pizza. Photograph: Hanif Sindhi.

8
Silk sari printed by the *patri* technique. Black & White collection designed by Archana Shah and launched in her store Bandhej in 1985. Photograph: M.P. Ranjan.

9
View of a kite shop during the Kite Festival. Photograph: Arvind Caulagi.

food and mutant versions of national and international cuisine has come to be the Ahmedabadi's passion (figure 7). Bhatt's essay surveys the Ahmedabadi's insatiable appetite for gastronomic variety and novelty and the simultaneous increase in gastric problems and proliferation of both weight-loss clinics and alternative therapies for restoring good health. These modern trends are presented against the city's Jain and Vaishnava traditions in observing strict food restrictions and fasting which have given Ahmedabad a seemingly overwhelming vegetarian ethos contrasted by widely prevalent meat eating in Muslim and working-class predominant areas.

The Ahmedabadi passion for the good life is sustained by material prosperity which was traditionally based on the city's vibrant textile traditions – explored in the next essay by textile designer Aditi Ranjan (figure 8). Nourished and nurtured by the waters of the Sabarmati were the city's blockmakers, dyers, printers, and washermen who were not only skilled craftsmen but artists in their manipulation of form and colour and scientists who understood the chemistry of dyes as well as the biology of plants, trees, and insects. Their mastery was matched by the business acumen of Ahmedabadi merchants who financed and managed a lucrative subcontinental and transcontinental textile trade which spanned

10
Muharram procession with *tazia*s moving through the city streets in 1937, by Pranlal Patel.

the two ends of the Indian Ocean – from East Asia to West Africa. Hand-printed cotton textile traditions managed to survive despite the expansion of mill-manufactured cloth in the late 19th century, and along with Gandhi's movement to promote khadi during the freedom struggle years. The question of their survival now looms large as hand processes become increasingly expensive and people's tastes are altered by the offerings in malls.

The late 1960s revealed a more disquieting side of Ahmedabad – the first major Hindu-Muslim riot in post-Independence India took place here in 1969 just as the city was preparing to celebrate the centenary of Gandhi's birth. This was followed by caste-based violence in the 1980s and communal violence again in the 1990s and in the early years of the new millennium. Yet, seemingly paradoxically, the crafts of Ahmedabad are a site for Hindu-Muslim synthesis. This is highlighted in designer and historian Suchitra Balasubrahmanyan's essay, which describes how kitemaking and the manufacture of traditional books of accounts bring together Hindu and Muslim communities in economic symbiosis, through ritual, or for sheer enjoyment (figure 9). Both crafts have been present in Ahmedabad probably since its inception and both involve paper, a material Ahmedabad was famous for manufacturing since medieval times.

The theme of overlaying, explored in the first essay, forms the leitmotif of the final essay by architect and researcher Yatin Pandya, which offers a view of the city as palimpsest (figures 1 and 10). Starting with the earliest phase of the city and bringing it up to the present, Pandya shows how each phase builds upon the earlier one, pointing out continuities and departures, footprints and erasures. Illustrated through the remarkable photographs of the eminent Ahmedabadi Pranlal Patel, who is now over a hundred years old, the concluding essay offers an eloquent glimpse of 20th-century Ahmedabad, setting the stage for the most crucial of questions – where does the city go from here?

The completion of 600 years is a moment to pause, to look back so that one can look forward. On the one hand it is a moment of nostalgia as Ahmedabadis are campaigning vigorously for the city's medieval core to be recognized as a UNESCO World Heritage Site. On the other hand, modern townplanning methods are ensuring that the city's limits extend and spread in all directions with ring roads, flyovers, and a bus rapid transport system, so that the city can be acknowledged as a true megacity. The river which once offered sustenance to the city is now being lined with concrete so as to offer modern entertainment and livelihood as well the opportunity for real-estate development on the reclaimed riverbanks. The 600th anniversary of Ahmedabad's foundation is a significant milestone and a fitting occasion to review aspects of its past and view its present. This milestone is both a time for celebration and for reflection in order to provide a context to ponder over what lies ahead for the city and its people. This is what the present volume hopes to accomplish.

Acknowledgements
Ahmedabad 600: Portraits of a City is a very special volume for us. It is our tribute to the city which has shaped us in many ways – as students, as young adults, as professionals.

We could not have brought out this volume without the help and support of many friends and colleagues. Our grateful thanks to Shridhar Andhare who placed intuitive trust in us and introduced us to the team at Marg; and to Rashmi Poddar who responded warmly to his suggestion and invited us to visualize this volume.

Later, our new friends at Marg helped and supported us through the process, gently nudging us towards deadlines and cheerfully accommodating our teaching commitments at CEPT. We could not have worked on this volume without the help of our colleagues at the Faculty of Arts and Humanities, particularly Nasarin Bhojani, and our students who reversed roles and gave us a lesson or two in digital technologies.

To all the writers, photographers, and mapmakers, our warmest thanks for bringing their insights and images to this volume and for revealing to us unknown aspects of a city we thought we already knew so well.

Architectural Traditions
of the Evolving City

R.J. Vasavada

Several scholars have written about Ahmedabad's history that dates back to the early 15th century. Their records reflect various socio-political phases, each of which left its imprint on the evolution of the city. The early influences were clearly of the Gujarat Sultanate, which established the city in the 15th century and ruled over it for the next one and a half centuries, until replaced by new and greater powers. The city rose to eminence and was considered to be one of the finest in the subcontinent with its beautiful built environment and the affluence of its people. The richness and artistry of its settlements, monuments, and religious buildings impressed and were appreciated by travellers from across the country and abroad, several of whom wrote accounts. Today Ahmedabad's architecture of temples, monuments, and domestic buildings remains a unique treasure representing the variety of its traditional cultures.

Regional Traditions
In the 10th and 11th centuries, prior to the founding of Ahmedabad, the region with Anhilwad-Patan (about 135 kilometres north of Ahmedabad, later known as just Patan; Anawada which was the original Anhilwad-Patan lies to the northwest of the present-day Patan town) as the capital of the Solanki rulers, witnessed a vibrant period of cultural richness, Jainism being the major religion. The Jain community, strongly bonded by religion, supported the building of exquisite temples dedicated to the *tirthankaras* in towns and cities. Several *tirtha*s (sacred sites), including temple cities, provided generous patronage to craftsmen and master-builders who employed their highest skills in the service of these religious edifices. Individual zeal for temple-building – as houses of gods – was reflected in equal measure in the treatment of domestic architecture. As a result, a very strong basis for an unprecedented tradition of settlement architecture was established in the region.

Tradition is a repository of beliefs and facts that are handed down over generations. Jain art and architecture are a substream of the mainstream Hindu cultural tradition. Jain artists and builders followed the mainstream practices and beliefs while positioning their own variations in art and architecture, which expressed the philosophy of their religion. The Jain temple became more elaborate and ornate in its expression while its utilitarian buildings remained closer to the mainstream tradition. The house, considered as an extension of the temple in the Jain understanding, provided another site for the expression of their penchant for religious art and architecture.

The building enterprises patronized by the Solanki rulers, including some magnificent temples and temple cities, introduced many contextually relevant building types such as stepwells, *kund*s (constructed water reservoirs) and various other tanks, and ceremonial archways, besides settlements and fortifications with imposing gateways in the cities and towns under their dominance. This was done as a measure for public good (*ishtapurta*), which was considered the duty of rulers. This positioning of architecture and art in the socio-political milieu was the approach that the Jain community followed and, as a result, artistic expression took very strong roots, lending identity to the community's culture and lifestyle.

The Jain building tradition thus became a product of their beliefs, situating architectural expression as a sum total of various aspects such as the symbolic, the spatial, the formal, as well as the technical. The canonical texts which the master-builders used in Jain temple-building were reinterpreted from the mainstream Hindu texts in order to achieve a form of temple which was true to their philosophy. The ideas of multiplicity of worship within the Jain religion became the basis of form, with the symbol of *meru* (mountain, pillar of the universe) being the most important as the ultimate *tirtha*. Several important temples are located on hills and are known as *tuk* (hill-top).

The entire spectrum of the building arts and sciences was a result of the ingenuity of a very vast community of master-builders and craftsmen, who were amongst the best and were amply patronized by the rulers and nobility in Solanki times. The body of beliefs and knowledge they followed and interpreted was enshrined in the canonical texts which dealt with all the aspects of building, including engineering and technology. The texts also covered the earth sciences of soil, natural materials, and quarrying. With the help of this knowhow, the techniques of building engineering and construction were perfected and practised. The system of construction and the structure were conceived in perfect harmony with natural laws of balance.

The temples were richly carved and adorned with sculptures dedicated to the deities, the guardian angels, and the cardinal angels in such a manner as to convey their symbolic representation of the universe. Jain temples dedicated to tirthankaras reflected their presence in icons with relevant imagery that narrated examples of righteous living and conduct in keeping with the religion and its dictates, which worshippers should follow. They also provided a place for discourses – the *mandapa* (pavilion), an important element of the temple form. The *mandapa* with 12 pillars – three in each corner – was the most perfected simple form of construction, which was elaborated into a structure with 14 pillars in each corner, totalling 56, as temples grew larger in size. This simple form of supports evolved into the octagonal support structure to facilitate the construction of roofs in successive tiers of flat beams and plates rising in projected, corbelled pyramidal roofs known as *shamran*. The main *shikhara* (temple spire) or the roof over the sanctum was only a manifestation of the construction of walls closing inwards from the four sides, sealed at the top with a finial stone. There could be nothing more in tune with nature, achieving the most symbolic of all forms pointing upwards to the worship of the Supreme nature, the giver of all life.

The house was conceived as a self-contained unit providing all living needs. The conception of domestic buildings followed the religious philosophy in treating the house as a temple, but varied in its form and structure. The materials used for domestic buildings were timber and brick, which were more accessible. For this reason the pattern of tiered horizontal construction was commonly followed in devising the structure of houses. Timber replaced stone in domestic architecture for its flexibility and affordability, while still providing ample freedom for adornment and carving. Perfect balance and harmony were achieved through the use of standard dimensions in the construction of facades and supports, composite with masonry construction, which also allowed flexibility in modification of the structures. Timber was also a humane material suited to domestic settlement and the wooden street facade created a very comfortable living environment in the dry, hot climate of the region.

The house which was a constituent of the settlement known as a "pol", was seen as an independent self-sufficient unit within the settlement in terms of its form and substance.

1
Study of a typical house and its perceived meanings in architecture. Drawing: author, 1984.

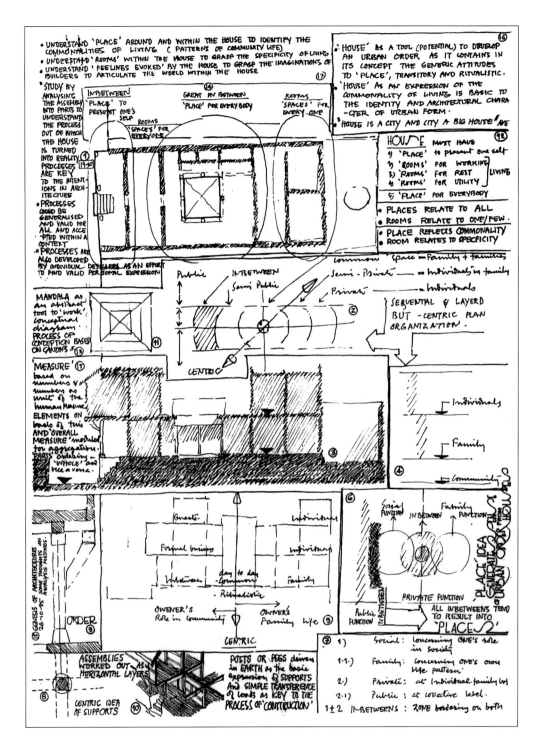

A traditional house in the city was designed around a court. The court provided the element of nature within the tight-knit house. Besides providing natural light and ventilation, the court also had an underground storage tank which collected the rainwater that ran off the roofs and terraces for year-round usage; this was a common feature of all pol houses. The court was the essential core of the house, providing the rooms around it exposure to the open air. Appropriately, the wooden facade of the court was very richly carved with representations of nature and all forms of life crowding the surfaces of the timber elements. The various representations of flora and fauna and mythical stories virtually created a reflection of the universe within the world of the house. The house was thus conceived as a reflection of the world outside and the universe beyond, through the aperture of the court open to the sky. This was one of the most significant

2
Cluster of houses inside a pol in the Kalupur area of the historic city. Photograph: P.M. Dalwadi, 1979.

expressions achieved through its design and execution. The house was thus a world within a world.

Houses shared common sidewalls with their neighbours and offered a very humane street front with a projecting wooden facade, which shaded the street and included an elevated pillared veranda. The entire wooden facade enveloping the front of all the floors was wonderfully constructed, projecting further outwards at each floor, shading the lower

3
A haveli in the same pol in the Kalupur area, with a doorway to the main street on the left.
Photograph: P.M. Dalwadi, 1979.

floor. The ornate pillars on the ground-floor veranda had very delicately carved brackets that supported the projecting upper floors. The entire schema of woodcarving defining various structural parts and elements had symbolic connotations of cultural identity as well as of the rich craft traditions, with the craftsmen offering their excellent skills and imagination to provide an expression which has few parallels in other urban settings of this kind. The facades were an important aspect of the pol, which was the hub of community life. The entire settlement with several pols made up the historic city's form, with communities settled in their own domestic structures enjoying a complete social environment rarely found in other cities of those times.

The most unique building type of this tradition is related to water. Several stepwells (*vav*s, *vapi*s) and reservoirs in the form of large manmade tanks (*talao*s) were built in towns and cities as a benevolent measure by the kings and the nobility during this period. The stepwell, in the form of a stepped corridor interspersed with pavilions, was built as an extension to a well, tapping underground streams as a source of water. Unfortunately there is only one surviving example of this period in Ahmedabad: the Mata Bhavani Vav located in Asarwa area, which was built presumably in Karan Vaghela's period during the 11th century. Of the same period, the stepwell at Patan known as Rani ki Vav is the largest and most ornate of such structures. This stepwell was built by Queen Udaymati in memory of her husband King Bhimdev. Near this well is the largest tank known as Sahasralinga Talao, also built in the 11th century. The tank was created by an ingenious system of diverting water from the nearby Sarasvati river, an early example of water management and irrigation for public good. The sides of the tank were detailed with a series of embankments and steps on which scores of small shrines sprang up, turning this source of water into a place of reverence.

All these building types and their adornments reflected strong linkages to traditional belief systems. Master-builders extended their skills with equal ease to different types of buildings and also dedicated themselves with religious zeal to excel in all their enterprises, which made the tradition stronger and rooted in the culture which patronized them. The architectural art of the 11th-century Solanki era was the fountainhead of all the later developments in the architecture of Ahmedabad and Gujarat. This was the tradition that strongly influenced every incoming ruler, leading them to adjust their own practices and preferences to this dominant context.

Architecture under Sultanate Rule
The new architectural expression that developed in the 15th century drew its strength from the already established dominant tradition of this region. The incoming Sultanate rulers indulged in plundering the existing edifices of immense architectural value and, it is believed, employed the same fragments in their own structures built for religious and other purposes. The use of parts plundered from temples resulted in a form of Sultanate building which greatly deviated from their own methods of construction and conception of the resultant space. The mosque became a pillared hall (like the 12-pillared *mandapa* of the temple) with only the addition of the dome, which was lifted on pillars admitting light within – "clear-storey lighting". The dome, central to Islamic monuments, was in the earlier mosques of Ahmedabad merely a replica of the corbelled, horizontal layered construction seen in local Jain temples. The dome was thus never a true dome but the already perfected corbelled mandapa ceiling so characteristic of temples. This was a major local influence on the Sultanate mosque, which otherwise is a simple masonry-construction hall with domes, with squinches or stalactite pendentives at the interior corners. The features of Sultanate architecture from its own context and traditions were expressed only partially through the facades where minarets and large pointed arched openings were introduced. These were the only elements which resembled the Islamic idiom. The mihrab, which is the focus while offering prayers within the mosque, was extremely richly carved by local craftsmen, with the exception of the cusp of the pointed arch – a symbolic representation of hands folded in prayer.

As part of mosques, the minarets became the central attraction due to the form and resilience of their constructional techniques. Minaret decoration was greatly influenced by the talent of the local craftsmen, who excelled in stonecarving and statuary. Though the craftsmen followed their own choices of motifs and patterns, there was a complete departure from their preference for natural representation, in keeping with the tenets of Islam. Islamic philosophy accepts geometric patterns of lines and colour, but never plastic forms and imitation of nature in art. This was a major influence on local practices and artistic interpretations in the Sultanate period in Ahmedabad. Fine sculptural art with excellently crafted stonework was the hallmark of work achieved by craftsmen under Sultanate patronage, and drew the attention of critics and art lovers from all over the world in later times, including historians such as James Burgess, Jas Burgess, Theodore Hope, James Fergusson, and Percy Brown.

The architecture of mosques and tombs in Ahmedabad represents thus a unique idiom that developed out of the acceptance of influences from the local traditions by the emerging Sultanate styles. This gave rise to a very distinct expression in what is later known as the Indo-Saracenic architecture of western India, a result of the fusion of two diverse concepts in architecture, which were a product of distinctly different cultures. Islamic traditions, essentially Arabic in nature, were brought in by the Sultanate rulers, and were immensely influenced by the local idiom and artistry of Indian craftsmen and master-builders. These artists were completely at ease working for the Sultanate rulers, who allowed their skills a completely free hand. They achieved glory through their masterful creations for rulers who represented a completely different cultural ethos. Ahmedabad's multicultural identity took deep root in these times and as a result socio-political enterprises flourished during the 15th century under Ahmed Shah, placing Ahmedabad at the forefront of cities in India. This later attracted the attention of the Mughal empire.

Local building types such as stepwells also influenced the Sultanate rulers, and they continued the building type in which they found cool retreats for their own use. They reinterpreted this type into several such subterranean buildings in and around Ahmedabad,

4
A typical court as a central open space within a haveli in the Kalupur area of the historic city.
Photograph: P.M. Dalwadi, 1979.

5
Detail of a haveli facade with wooden construction of post and bracket. Photograph: P.M. Dalwadi, 1979.

for example Bhammaria Kua, the helical well at Muhammadabad. Dada Hari Vav and Adalaj Vav, both built in the late 15th century, are two of the most important stepwells in this region. The practice of building stepwells continued in later times and several such structures were added. Lakes and tanks were also constructed around the city, with an extensive network of catchment and waste weirs involving elaborate systems of ornate stone structures for restraining the water flow and extensive stepped embankments for people to access the waterfront. The Gujarat Sultans also brought in a system of irrigation for the

  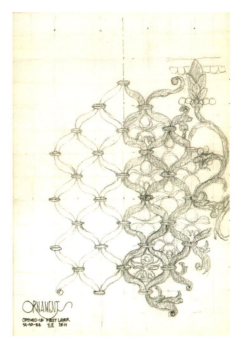

6
Sketch showing ornate details of a bracket in a haveli. Observe the intricacy of carving depicting a floral creeper pattern as a wrap around the solid core of wood. Drawing: author, 1984.

7
Sketch of the same bracket showing the core. Drawing: author, 1984.

8
Sketch of the intricate floral creeper pattern. Drawing: author, 1984.

Bhadra Fort area and Azam Khan's Sarai, with a waterwheel constructed near Ganesh Bari (present east end of Ellis Bridge) which drew river water to the top of the bastion and then through a channel network over the southern fort wall all the way to the palace.

An important element which was brought in by the Sultanate rulers was the concept of open spaces and gardens as part of their city-planning exercise. The Maidan e Shahi between the Bhadra ramparts and the Three Gates was the major public place in front of the entrance to the Fort, which was the main access to the palace. The Maidan was entered from the city through the Three Gates. Important monuments like the Jami Masjid and kings' and queens' tombs are situated at the intersection of the city's main east-west and north-south thoroughfares. The city gates and the Fort were certainly characteristic forms of Sultanate building enterprise from their indigenous culture, and exhibit grandeur and impressive forms in masonry construction.

Domestic architecture during the Sultanate period integrated very well within the overall settlement character of the city. The areas known as *pur* (settlement) were distinctly separate for different communities. (The nomenclature *pur* was common in the local language which had already accepted a lot of Arabic words within its vocabulary as a result of trade. The term used locally for a domestic settlement is pol.) The Muslim communities, depending on their economic occupations, lived in separate settlements within the city. Thus the trading and merchant communities were settled in the northeastern parts known as Kalupur, while those involved in crafts and textiles settled in the southwest of the city obviously due to its proximity to the riverbed. There was a unique closeness and harmonious coexistence among the various communities due to a tremendous sharing of economic interests in trade and commerce. This rich multicultural character of urban life was an important aspect of Ahmedabad and made it a very prosperous centre of that period in the subcontinent.

Settlement and house forms in Ahmedabad had a distinct character, a result of people's strong adherence to the lifestyle ordained by their religious traditions, which regulated their community bondage and their daily life. The two main communities, Jain and Muslim, both had this unifying bondage which was expressed in their settlement patterns and house forms. The physical character of the house form differed only marginally in terms of its relation to the street or pol. But the use of material for construction and the basic form adopted were very similar as these were controlled by the availability of local building materials and climatic considerations for comfortable living conditions.

As in the earlier period, the typical Muslim house was planned around a court as the important inner element. The house also had a *tanka* (underground tank) to store rainwater as was the normal practice here, and was a self-sufficient living unit. The functional areas within the house differed significantly according to the Muslim lifestyle. The external element of the veranda was minimized to the position of an entrance. The front areas were a buffer between the outer and inner sections as there was a distinct sense of privacy, and the inner court was selectively exposed. The upper storeys of the facade were also more secured and private. The facades were relatively less ornate when it came to Muslim settlements, though the general treatment did reflect the prevailing craft traditions of wooden architecture which had a very distinct character. The carvings displayed Muslim choices and preferences for symbolism with their own religion.

What distinctly differed at settlement level is the way Muslim communities organized their social life. The mosque – a place for community worship as well as a meeting place – occupied an important position at the entrance of the pol. Among the Bohras – a significant Muslim merchant community – the settlement had a community hall adjoining the mosque for all community-related functions. In contrast, among Jains and Hindus, the temple and the community-related functions were always situated at the heart of the pol settlement, in an open space such as a public square.

Evolving Traditions

Architectural traditions are nurtured by the socio-political context at a given time. The art and science of architecture are governed by the attitudes within a culture. These attitudes are reflected through the approach to the symbolic, spatial, formal, and technical aspects of architecture within the larger context of the prevailing culture. While the art and science of building offer methods and techniques to realize the structures, symbolic and functional attributes qualify their appearance and appropriateness, resulting in a cultural expression. This is how buildings of the past can be "read" as cultural symbols and thus have a bearing on ongoing tradition, making historical architectural works a repository of "cultural heritage" for succeeding generations.

The architectural expression of a culture is shaped very importantly by the people who directly deal with the production of buildings – traditionally the master-builders and craftsmen. They were organized as communities with their own systems of acquiring hereditary skills and abilities, besides knowledge of the texts (including compendiums on architecture, iconography, sculpture, and carving) along with common-sense wisdom, which they inherited and transmitted down the generations through practice and apprenticeships. These master-builders and craftsmen presented themselves as a guild, irrespective of their own personal religious affinities; most important were their skills and abilities in the particular building trade at which they excelled. These guilds were the torchbearers of an ongoing tradition. Through their excellence in their trade the traditions evolved in time and were nurtured with new vigour each time there was a breakthrough in conception and practice. This is clearly observed in the case of influences brought by the merchant communities having overseas trade relations. The prominent influence came from European traders, who brought in imagery from their countries which the local traders adopted as new decorative elements for their houses, showing their status. The guilds worked on building enterprises proposed by any patron and were mainly concerned with finding appropriate opportunities for work and exhibiting their talents. They were free to express their skills once the basic concepts were accepted. Whenever new patrons emerged as rulers or employers, there was a constant sharing, exchange, and a newer amalgam within the ongoing tradition. This was also the reason for the emergence of successive influenced traditions and the vitality and vigour of new expressions. Sultanate and Mughal influences followed by European influences are clearly visible when one examines the historic fabric of the old city.

Traditions in an ongoing cultural flow always emerge or get strengthened out of the beliefs of the people and are supported by the increasing knowhow in an advancing or shifting cultural scenario. In Ahmedabad this aspect is very evident and operative. Every new epoch of changing leadership has infused a new amalgam as explained above, a result of newer expression growing out of the existing context which influences the incoming political leadership. This constant renewal and redefining has been a very strong factor in keeping the traditions alive and pulsating. Considering Ahmedabad's history, its strength has been in keeping the strong identity of its earlier traditions alive and potent enough to provide sufficient flexibility and freedom for others to absorb their contents, and to nurture other cultures without losing its inherent identity. This was also possible through the talent and expertise of its communities of master-builders and crafts guilds, who continuously worked towards excellence and innovation with full understanding of the limits set by their varied patrons, and still adhering to the substance and meaning of their own traditions. Shifting cultural flows were very ably negotiated by these communities of master-builders and craftsmen and high standards of excellence in traditional art and architecture were sustained by them in spite of socio-political changes and the diverse demands imposed by the changing patronage.

9
A typical street in the Dariyapur area of the historic city, dominated by Muslim communities, showing the evolving trends in the first half of the 20th century with changing attitudes to materials and structure. Photograph: author, 2011.

The traditional architecture of Ahmedabad sustained its character until the end of the Sultanate period. It subsequently fell into oblivion as a result of political uncertainties and diminishing control by the Mughals. The city subsequently came under the Marathas and then finally under British rule. This is when new methods in construction and usage of materials totally alien to the traditional system started substituting for the earlier strengths of evolving traditions. These changes influenced the construction and treatment of the houses in the historic city. In the initial phases such influences were confined to accepting new materials and techniques of construction of houses, keeping the house plans unaffected, and carrying on the traditional lifestyles. What was marginally affected was the sense of scale of the houses, but the harmonious character of the facades and streetscapes was still maintained, differing only in the imagery which reflected new motifs and new materials.

With colonial rule taking over the regional administration and controls, the traditional skills were looked down upon as archaic, to be suppressed, with Western techniques and materials being introduced to bring the "modernity" of the industrial age into a culture which was attempting to free itself from oblivion and decay. The culture, instead of trying to rediscover itself, went in the direction of completely transforming itself, with a new breed of "industrialists" led by Western attitudes and preferences qualified to living under British rule. The leaders of communities, trying to please their colonial rulers, started adopting Western-style house facades. This later was reflected in their choice

10
An early 20th-century mosque in the Dariyapur area of the historic city illustrates the changing influences on the architecture of mosques. Photograph: author, 2011.

of lifestyle, and a completely new trend of suburban living began to be adopted, with "progressive" new forms of buildings – both institutional as well as domestic – known as "bungalows", being built in plotted land developments across the river. The first of such bungalows came up on the fringes of the old city wall on the west side, and then in the suburbs that had begun growing on the west of the old city across Ellis Bridge, which is known today as Pritam Nagar. This development became the starting point of a complete makeover of the historic city's traditional fabric, replacing all the earlier evolving strands in a British-engineered breakthrough for the "Western" city in the early 20th century. The city thereafter has grown in successive decades into its present state with more and more influences coming from Europe and America, along with the pressures placed upon it by an increasing population and "development".

References

Amar, Gopilal, "Architectural Traditions and Canons", in A. Ghosh (ed.), *Jaina Art and Architecture*, Vol. III, Part IX, New Delhi: Bharatiya Jnanpith, 1974.
Brown, Percy, *Indian Architecture (Buddhist and Hindu Periods)*, reprint, Bombay: Taraporevala and Sons, 1976.
Burgess, Jas, *The Muhammadan Architecture of Ahmedabad*, reprint, New Delhi: ASI, 1997.
Dhaky, M.A. (ed.), *Hutheesing Heritage: The Jain Temple at Ahmedabad*, Ahmedabad: Hutheesing Kesrising Trust, 1998.
Fergusson, James, *Architecture at Ahmedabad: The Capital of Goozerat*, London: John Murray, 1866.
Fergusson, James, *History of Indian and Eastern Architecture*, Vol. II, reprint, Delhi: Munshiram Manoharlal, 1967.
Gillion, Kenneth L., *Ahmedabad: A Study in Indian Urban History*, Ahmedabad: New Order Book Company, 1968.
Jain, S.P., *Social Structure of Hindu-Muslim Community*, Delhi: National Publishing House, 1975.
Jain-Neubauer, Jutta, *Stepwells of Gujarat in Art-Historical Perspective*, New Delhi: Abhinav Publications, 1981.
Khan, Ali Muhammad, M.F. Lokhandwala (trans.), *Mirat-i-Ahmadi: A Persian History of Gujarat*, Baroda: Oriental Institute, 1965.
Michell, George and Snehal Shah (eds.), *Ahmadabad*, reprint, Mumbai: Marg Publications, 2003.
Shah, Umakant P., *Studies in Jaina Art*, Ahmedabad: Jain Cultural Research Society, 1955.
Shah, U.P. and M.A. Dhaky, *Aspects of Jaina Art and Architecture*, Gujarat State Committee for the Celebration of 2500th Anniversary of Bhagavan Mahavira Nirvana, Ahmedabad: L.D. Institute of Indology, 1975.
Trivedi, R.K., "Wood Carving of Gujarat", *Census of India 1961*, Vol. V, Gujarat, Part VII (2), Ahmedabad: Gujarat Census Publications, 1965.
Trivedi, R.K., "Special Report on Ahmedabad City", *Census of India 1961*, Vol. V, Gujarat, Ahmedabad: Gujarat Census Publications, 1967.

Ahmedabad as a Centre of Painting

Shridhar Andhare

The heritage of Ahmedabad goes back to its ancestral town, Patan (c. 746 CE), known as Anhilwad Patan or Devaka Pattana (Sanskrit) in early Jain literature. Patan grew from the 8th to the 14th centuries on the strength of its position as a regional capital city and the most vital trading centre of western India. It enjoyed the special reputation of being a culturally prosperous town, where the breathtaking Rani ki Vav (Queen's Stepwell) was created, and is acknowledged as the pinnacle of sculptural art of the 11th century (figure 1). It was Patan where revered Jaina *acharya*s like Hemachandracharya and others lived and propagated Jainism to the masses.

Jain *Shastra Bhandar*s

The upsurge of Jainism in Gujarat, and Patan in particular, is largely attributed to the tradition of *shastra dan*, the gifting of religious books to secure spiritual merit, which was considered a virtuous act among Jains. This idea of reverence for learning was the main inspiration in the creation of *shastra bhandar*s, repositories of manuscripts on religious and secular subjects, both illustrated and otherwise. Although it is difficult to date the inception of this tradition of creating *shastra bhandar*s, it is likely to have begun after the Vallabhi convention of the 5th or 6th century when it was decided to record the oral traditions in writing. The next stage was the production of religious books by Jain monks who presented their valuable contributions to various Jain *bhandar*s all over Gujarat.

Two great patrons of the art of the book were the kings of Patan – Jaisimha Siddharaj (1094–1143) and Kumarapal (1143–74). Siddharaj employed 300 scribes to copy books while Kumarapal, it is said, established 21 *shastra bhandar*s and presented each one of them with a copy of the *Kalpasutra* written in gold ink.[1]

The Shift to Ahmedabad

With the Muslim invasion of the 13th century, Patan's prosperous and extensive trade and commerce was severely disturbed and its pre-eminence was further eclipsed by the shifting of the capital to Ahmedabad in 1411, by Ahmed Shah. From then onwards the regional focus shifted to Ahmedabad.

There was a great impetus to mosque-building activity in Ahmedabad and a number of magnificent stone edifices with exquisite trellis work of Indian and Islamic motifs sprang up in and around the city. Prominent among them were stepwells, mosques, and mausoleums built during Sultan Mahmud Begada's reign (1458–1511). His fondest site was the Roza of Sarkhej, a complex of superb artistic buildings with a manmade reservoir at the centre surrounded by tombs and mosques built later during the Mughal period. The centre of attraction was the tomb of the saint Sheikh Ahmed Khattu Ganj Baksh (c. 14th century). Its domical structure has bands of concentric circles on the inside with paintings

1
Sculptures from Rani ki Vav, Patan, Gujarat, c. 11th century.
Photograph: Anand Patel.

of floral patterns and Persian clouds which point to the style of painting of the Sultanate period of Ahmedabad. Building activity seemed to recede after the construction of the stepwell of Adalaj (c. 15th century).

The Jains however continued their temple-building activity at famous pilgrimage centres like Palitana, Shatrunjaya, Girnar, Mount Abu, Ranakpur, and many other picturesque locations in western India. A situation of tolerance and pluralism prevailed in Ahmedabad, and there was ample scope for all religions to thrive to a greater or lesser extent. The Vaishnavas (followers of the cult of Srinathji at Nathdwara), the Shaktas (followers of Devi or the divine goddess), and the followers of the Swaminarayan sect were free to pursue their respective religions. Several of the Swaminarayan temples all over Gujarat are decorated profusely with mythological and other scenes painted by local or itinerant artists in the late 19th or early 20th century.

Jain Miniatures

The seed of miniature painting was sown at Patan in the medieval period with the Jain manuscript tradition, but its style remained stereotyped, rigid, and repetitive for several centuries thereafter. Stylistically, with its two-dimensional and flat treatment, it developed its own characteristics of pointed nose, double chin, and the farther eye protruding into space, wherein the red monochrome colour dominated. The extreme sanctity and security bestowed by the Jains upon these sacred religious documents, preserved in Jain *bhandar*s, enabled monks and scholars to continue in-depth study and research.

In the middle of the 20th century, the outstanding contribution of one of the most revered Jain monks and scholars of the Shvetambara sect, Muni Sri Punyavijayji, was recognized by Kasturbhai Lalbhai, a devout Jain *shreshthi* (merchant) and textile magnate of Ahmedabad. Kasturbhai was a renowned patron of art too, and a lucky confluence of Lakshmi (goddess of wealth) and Sarasvati (goddess of learning) took place in the coming together of *dhana* (wealth) and *vidya* (learning), leading to the establishment of the L.D. Institute of Indology at Ahmedabad in 1964. Exactly 20 years later, a new building came up by the side of the mother institution as the L.D. Museum, to house paintings, sculptures, and other artefacts. This museum now holds some of the most valuable Jain and non-Jain treasures of the country.

Painting in Ahmedabad

From a closer look at the history of painting in Gujarat as a whole and Ahmedabad's contribution in particular, it will be apparent that painting remained a catalytic agency which boosted art in all its forms. Though not geographically, but economically and culturally Ahmedabad remained a focal point from where art seems to have been disseminated. The *vihara*, or movement of Jain *muni*s (monks) from one town to another, meant that they required portable painted artefacts from time to time for their rituals and religious ceremonies. Members of the laity commissioned the required paintings and manuscripts from painters and calligraphers as an act of piety which gave them spiritual merit. These materials were later collected and preserved at various *bhandar*s. The antiquarian written materials in the L.D. Institute's collection indicate a chronological development from the 11th century to the 19th century. The painted wooden book cover of *Jinadatta Suri* (figure 2) datable to the 12th century and the *Vidyadevi Patli* of the same date[2] can be regarded as the earliest examples of Jain painting. Palm-leaf manuscripts continued to be produced along with paper manuscripts which were introduced a little later, and a handful of this material has been published earlier.[3] During the 13th and the 14th centuries there was a tremendous proliferation of illustrated manuscripts and painted *pata*s or cloth paintings.

2
Part of a painted wooden book cover of *Jinadatta Suri*, western Indian style, c. 12th century. Collection of L.D. Museum, Ahmedabad.

Till about 1475 the style did not change, but thereafter we come to a landmark with the unique manuscript of the Devsano Pado *Kalpasutra* and *Kalakacharya Katha* (figure 3) which exhibits a combination of Persian and Jain elements in style for the first time. It is believed that the manuscript is now in the possession of a jeweller's family in Ahmedabad. The peculiarity of the painting style of the manuscript is that it departs from the stereotypical idea and concept of Jain painting. The artist seems to have been free to indulge in full-page illustrations with intricate border decorations, with a variety of landscapes, hunting scenes, floral sprays, and other interesting subjects. The ethnic types are depicted wearing large Bokhara turbans and long *jama*s (upper garments) while women are invariably shown with pointed waists and long, single plaits. A number of illustrated manuscripts dating from a slightly later period (1525–75) were discovered which are now called the Sultanate manuscripts.[4] These included new themes such as Islamic or Sufi poetic works, Indian epics, Ragamalas, and Hindu romances which had not been known earlier.

3
Kalaka Retrieving the Ball, folio from a *Kalpasutra* and *Kalakacharya Katha* manuscript, western Indian style, c. 1475. Formerly in the Devsano Pado Bhandar, Ahmedabad.

4
Krishna and the Gopas Playing a Game of Ball, folio from the *Bala Gopala Stuti*, western Indian style, c. 1450. Collection not known.

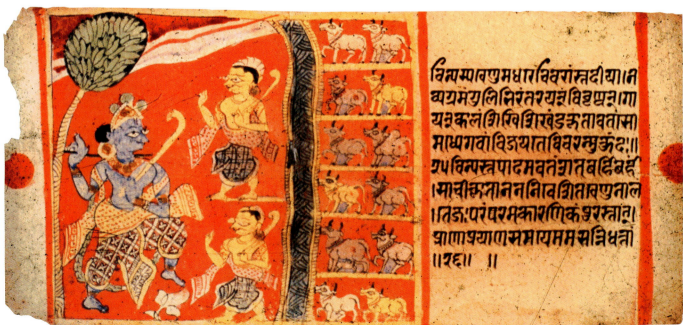

Shridhar Andhare

5
Folio from the *Vasanta Vilasa* scroll on cloth, western Indian style, painted at Ahmedabad in 1451. Collection of the Freer Gallery of Art, Smithsonian Institution, Washington DC.

However, at the time when the Jain-dominated Sultanate style was widespread in Gujarat, the painters' guilds and *laiya*s (calligraphers) in Gujarat also catered to the needs of the Vaishnavas. A number of c. 14th-century Vaishnava manuscripts of the *Bala Gopala Stuti* (Krishna's childhood exploits) composed by Bilvamangala exist, today scattered all over the world (figure 4). Stylistically and artistically they appear to be in Jain style but their contents refer to Vaishnava subjects.

Recalling the exuberance of the architectural activity of Ahmedabad in the Sultanate period, there was also painting activity on non-Jain subjects. Notable among these documents is a long and narrow cloth scroll of the *Vasanta Vilasa*[5] in Sanskrit which describes the beauty of the spring season (figure 5). Significantly, it includes a notation that it was painted at Ahmedabad in 1451 CE. Executed delicately in sophisticated Jain style, it is blooming with flora and fauna, showing forest landscapes with animals, and conveying the atmosphere of the season. Its ethnic types are carefully drawn and beautiful to look at. This phase of Ahmedabad painting is exemplary and unique. However, the old tradition of manuscript painting continued sporadically into the 17th and 18th centuries in smaller towns to which the Jain monks travelled and where they spent the *chaumasa* (the four months of the rainy season). Portable (*gutka*) manuscripts on socio-religious subjects in the literary forms of *katha, varta, doha, chaupai* were produced, mentioning dates, the places where they were created, and also the names of patrons who were Jain monks and sometimes *shresthi*s or merchants.[6]

It is pertinent here to briefly note some early developments in Mughal painting. According to the *Ain-i-Akbari*,[7] a number of painters were invited from all over India to work at the imperial studio, known as the *taswirkhana*, on the monumental project of the *Hamzanama*. Not only does it mention the names of the painters who worked on this project but it also refers to those who continued on the subsequent two important illustrated manuscripts of the *Razmnama* (the *Mahabharata*) and the *Ramayana*, now at the *pothikhana* at Jaipur. It is mentioned in this connection: "However, painters like Miskin, Dharamdas, and Sunawala who worked as assistants on the *Razmnama*, reached the peak of their form and a band of painters of considerable merit from Gujarat – Devji

6
Folio from the *Anwar-i-Suhaili*, painted at Ahmedabad in 1601. British Library, London.

7
Dancing and Music, a detail from the *Laghu Sangrahani Sutra*, painted at Matar in 1583. Collection of L.D. Museum, Ahmedabad.

Gujarati, Kesar Gujarati, Meghji Gujarati, Paramji Gujarati, and Surji Gujarati – joined the *taswirkhana* to assist the leading masters Basawan, Lal, Kesavdas, Mukund, and Mahesh."[8] And again, "Though there was no dearth of Gujarati painters in the Mughal *taswirkhana*, mention should be made of two Gujarati painters who were exposed to the Mughal court style directly or indirectly. The first is *Chitara* Govinda son of Narada, who visited Lahore where he first copied and illustrated the *Bhagavatapurana* in A.D. 1596."[9]

Another *Bhagavatapurana* and other Jain and Hindu works followed. One such Jain example entitled *Laghu Samgrahani Sutra* dated 1583 and painted at Matar (near Ahmedabad) has a folio mentioning the name of Chitara Govinda over the Siddhashila, while another similar manuscript of the *Uttaradhyayana Sutra* dated 1591[10] is preserved at the Museum and Picture Gallery at Vadodara.

The Mughal Impact

After Emperor Akbar's victory over Gujarat in 1573, the province was declared a *suba* (province) of Gujarat. Ahmedabad began to flourish rapidly, as there was peace and stability.[11] This, together with other factors such as availability of raw material and skilled labour in the city and the neighbouring rural areas, its comparative proximity to other parts of Gujarat, and its location on the trade route, helped in stimulating Ahmedabad's trade and manufacturing activities. In the late-Akbar and early-Jahangir period, there was an impact of Mughal culture and practices on the art, culture, religion, and trade and commerce of Gujarat in general and Ahmedabad in particular.

Mirza Aziz Koka, a high-ranking official of the Mughal court, was appointed governor of Gujarat and remained in charge from 1573 to 1575, from 1590 to 1593, from 1599 to 1605, and finally from 1601 to 1611 by proxy through his son. We find two important illustrated manuscripts of high quality produced during Aziz Koka's third spell of governorship. The first was Kashifi's book of fables called *Anwar-i-Suhaili* with 43 illustrations (figure 6), and the second was a copy of Sharfuddin Yazdi's Persian history of Timur known as *Zafarnama* with seven illustrations.[12] Both were prepared at Ahmedabad in AH 1009 (1600–01) and are presently in the collection of the British Library in London.

Mughal influence seems to have percolated into the Jain-oriented paintings of Gujarat in this phase. It appears that some painters of the royal studio at Delhi moved to Gujarat and Rajasthan in search of employment. This is evident from at least two illustrated manuscripts – the *Laghu Sangrahani Sutra* of 1583 painted at Matar[13] (Kheda district) by Chitara Govinda, presently in the collection of the L.D. Museum (figure 7), and the *Uttaradhyayana Sutra* of 1591,[14] now in the Museum and Picture Gallery, Vadodara. They display distinct Mughal elements in male and female costume and material culture. This trend mainly continued in the 17th-century manuscripts of *Sangrahani Sutra* now located in museums and private collections, as well as in the Jain monumental paintings (larger than the manuscript paintings) known from the Jain establishments.

Jain *Pata*s

Jains consider it customary to visit the *tirtha* (pilgrimage centre) of Shatrunjaya at least once in their lifetime to gain spiritual wisdom as this holy place is most sacred to them. For those unable to visit the *tirtha*, the Jains created a tradition of commissioning *pata*s or cloth paintings illustrating the *tirtha*s in symbolic and cartographic manner indicating the temples, buildings, lakes, and *kunda*s en route to the main shrine at the top of Shatrunjaya hill. A number of such *pata*s have been published by this writer.[15] These banners are hung, oriented towards the direction of Shatrunjaya hill, at sacred Jain locations such as

8
Vividha-tirtha-pata, painted on cloth at Ahmedabad in 1641. Collection of Samvegi Jain Upashraya, Ahmedabad. Photograph: Anand Patel.

8a
Detail of *vividha-tirtha-pata* showing Shatrunjaya *tirtha* and Girnar.

temples, *upashraya*s (temporary shelters for itinerant sadhus and sadhvis), and other such religious institutions on the day of the Kartik Punam, i.e. on the full moon day in the month of Kartik (October–November). From this day onwards the *tirtha* of Shatrunjaya is open to the public. Wealthy Jain families often commissioned such paintings, known as *tirtha-pata*s. Therefore we see a number of such banners of varying artistic merit in Jain *bhandar*s.

In 1985–86, a large exhibition of about a hundred or more Jaina *pata*s was held at the L.D. Museum in Ahmedabad. Among the displayed material, there were a couple of outstanding exhibits of historical as well as socio-religious significance. Both were *vividha-tirtha-pata*s[16] (banners displaying various Jain *tirtha*s). The first, measuring 4.54 x 1.20 metres, belonged to the Samvegi Jain Upashraya and the second measuring 3.54 x 1.08

8b
Detail of *vividha-tirtha-pata* showing temple courtyard.

8c
Detail of *vividha-tirtha-pata* showing pilgrims arriving via sea and land.

8d (opposite)
Detail of *vividha-tirtha-pata* showing auspicious symbols.

8e (opposite)
Detail of *vividha-tirtha-pata* showing part of the colophon.

PAINTING | 45

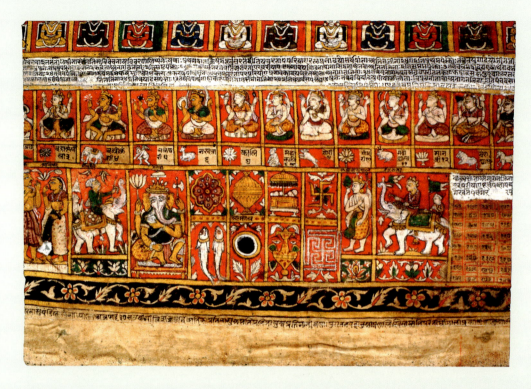

9a
Detail of *vividha-tirtha-pata*, painted on cloth at Ahmedabad in 1641. Collection of Anandji Kalyanji Pedhi, Ahmedabad.

9b
Detail showing the colophon of the *pata* from the Anandji Kalyanji Pedhi.

10
Detail of a 19th-century Shatrunjaya *pata* painted on cloth. Collection of Anandji Kalyanji Pedhi, Ahmedabad.

metres to the Anandji Kalyanji Pedhi, both in Ahmedabad (figures 8 and 9). Executed in a long and narrow format, both illustrate identical subject matter – various *tirtha*s – in a symbolic and cartographic form. They both possess extensive colophons, religious text, and numericals in Sanskrit. Each *tirtha* and object in the painting is labelled in Devanagari. They are profusely painted in red, orange, green, blue, yellow, and other colours in an aesthetic manner. Stylistically they appear to be close to the Mewar style of Rajasthani painting of the mid-17th century.

In the *pata* from the Pedhi, apart from the name of Sheth Shantidas of Ahmedabad, a Jain magnate of the Mughal period, there is mention of the succession of Jain monks, from Sri Hiravijayji[17] to Buddhi Sagar Suri and others, by whose command the *pata*s were commissioned by Sheth Shantidas. It is apparent from the substance of the colophons on the *pata*s that Sheth Shantidas was a devout Ahmedabadi Jain and spent his resources lavishly for religious purposes. His career and activities spanned the reigns of Mughal rulers from Akbar to Jahangir to Shahjahan to Aurangzeb and he had considerable influence at the imperial court at Delhi. Because of him the relationship between the Mughal authorities and the Jain monks was strengthened.[18]

Conclusion

It may be concluded that the two great *pata*s discussed above are not only representative of the art of painting in Ahmedabad in the middle of the 17th century but also remain pointers to the contemporary socio-religious activities of the Jains. We do observe a later continuity of the *pata* tradition but the verve, the aesthetic, and the overall style falls prey to the changing times (figures 10–12). A few large-size *pata*s were commissioned in Gujarat while some are known to have been made by the Mathen painters of Jodhpur and Bikaner. Subsequently, in the 19th and 20th centuries, the art seems to have shifted from Ahmedabad to Surat, a sea port on the southern tip of Gujarat.

Apart from the Jains, Muslim artists and professional craftsmen lived in Surat. They took to painting *tirtha-pata*s as well as cosmological charts etc. on the interior walls of Jain temples and on wooden panels, and made large-size *tirtha-pata*s on cloth. These *pata*s display contemporary culture in a bizarre manner, as one finds on the curtains and backdrops used in dramatic performances in vogue in those days. As a prominent centre of textiles and brocades, Ahmedabad had artisans who prepared *chode*s (backdrops and side curtains of the religious canopies from where Jain monks deliver religious discourses) for special occasions. These artefacts are usually made of expensive velvets adorned with heavy silver- and gold-brocade work. Such objects are often sponsored by Jain *sangha*s and display their names and dates as well as depictions of Jain themes such as the 14 dreams of Trishalamata (the mother of Mahavira) and the *ashtamangala*s, the eight auspicious symbols of the Jains.

Today, with modern technology and the pervasive spread of new materials and printing processes one would not be surprised to soon see *tirtha-pata*s made on polypropylene sheets of the sort used these days in commercial advertisements in public spaces in the city. Painters and calligraphers may be replaced by the computer and the place of the cloth *pata* may be taken by a new artefact with a new aesthetic.

Figure Acknowledgements
Unless otherwise credited, all photographs by Shridhar Andhare.

11
Shree Shatrunjaya Mahatirth *pata*, painted in oil on canvas in the early 20th century. Collection not known.

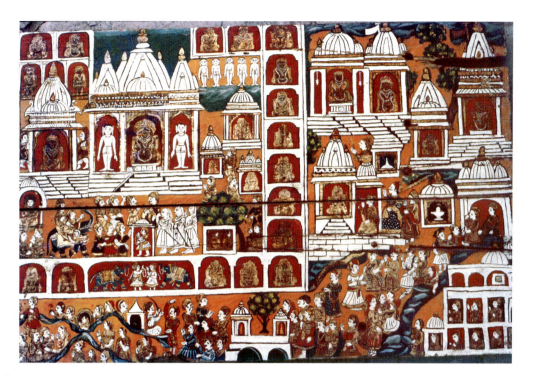

12
Detail of an early-20th-century *pata* on wood from Surat. Collection not known.

Notes

1. Moti Chandra, *Jain Miniature Painting from Western India*, Ahmedabad: Sarabhai Manilal Nawab, 1949, p. 3.
2. Muni Punyavijay and U.P. Shah, *Some Painted Wooden Book Covers from Western India*, Journal of the Indian Society of Oriental Art Special Number, Calcutta, 1965–66, col. pls. 3–5 and 11.
3. U.P. Shah, *Treasures of the Jain Bhandaras*, Ahmedabad: L.D. Series 69, 1978.
4. Karl Khandalavala and Moti Chandra, *New Documents of Indian Painting, A Reappraisal*, Bombay: Prince of Wales Museum, 1969, see colour plates.
5. Norman Brown, *The Vasanta Vilas*, New Haven: American Oriental Society, 1962.
6. Shah 1978, figs. 7 and 73–121; Moti Chandra and Umakant P. Shah, *New Documents of Jaina Paintings*, Bombay: Shri Mahavira Jaina Vidyalaya, 1975, groups V–VIII.
7. Abul Fazl, *Ain-i-Akbari* (trans H. Blochmann), Calcutta: The Asiatic Society, 1927, reprint 1993.
8. Asok Kumar Das, *Razmnama*, Calcutta and Ahmedabad: Birla Academy of Art and Culture in association with Mapin Publishing, 2008, p. 14.
9. Das 2008, pp. 14–15. Also see fn. 15 on p. 26.
10. Umakant P. Shah, *More Documents of Jaina Paintings and Gujarati Paintings of the Sixteenth and Later Centuries*, Ahmedabad: L.D. Series 51, 1976, figs. 41–43, 51, and 52.
11. Makrand Mehta, *Indian Merchants and Enterpreneurs in Historical Perspective*, Delhi: Academic Foundation, 1991, p. 93.
12. Das 2008, p. 24
13. Chandra and Shah 1975, col. pl. VIII folio 7b.
14. Shah 1976, figs 41–44.
15. Shridhar Andhare, "Jain Monumental Paintings", in Pratapaditya Pal (ed.), *The Peaceful Liberators: Jain Art from India*, Los Angeles: Los Angeles County Museum of Art, 1994, p. 77.
16. Shah 1978, see col. pls. V–VI. Also see Shridhar Andhare, "Painted Banners on Cloth: Vividha-tirtha-pata of Ahmedabad", in Mulk Raj Anand (ed.), *Homage to Kalamkari*, Bombay: Marg Publications, 1979, p. 40.
17. *Jain Rasamala* (Gujarati), Part 1, Srimad Buddhisagarji Granthamala No. 24, Bombay, 1902, p. 8. Also see Shridhar Andhare, "Imperial Mughal Tolerance of Jainism and Jain Painting Activity in Gujarat", in Rosemary Crill, Susan Stronge, and Andrew Topsfield (eds.), *Arts of Mughal India: Studies in Honour of Robert Skelton*, Ahmedabad: Mapin Publishing, 2004, pp. 223–33.
18. M.S. Commissariat, *A History of Gujarat (With a Survey of its Monuments and Inscriptions)*, Vol. 2, Bombay: Orient Longman, 1957, pp. 140–43.

Arabic-Persian Scholarship
Medieval Manuscripts at the Hazrat Pir Muhammad Shah Dargah Sharif Library

Mohaiuddin Bombaywala

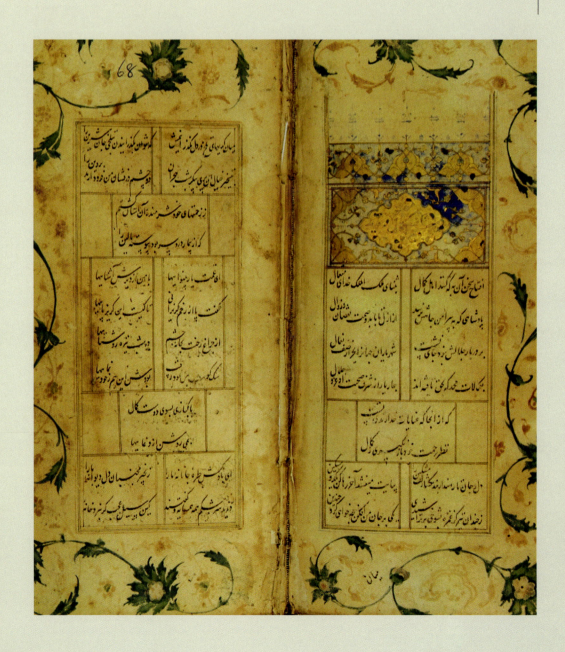

Ahmedabad is a prosperous centre of trade and commerce, renowned for its handwoven and blockprinted textiles, woodwork, exquisitely carved stone traceries or *jali*s, and innumerable other crafts. This mercantile and craft-manufacturing aspect has eclipsed an important facet of the city as a centre of Arabic and Persian scholarship in the 15th to 18th centuries. The story of Arabic and Persian scholarship in Ahmedabad can of course be pieced together from various literary sources such as *Hajji al-dabir, Mirat-i-Sikandari, Ain-i-Akbari, Jahangirnama*, and *Mirat-i-Ahmadi*. But a living testimony to the city's intellectual glory is the Hazrat Pir Muhammad Shah (HPMS) Dargah Sharif Library. Its extensive collection of medieval manuscripts, books, and inscriptions throws light on this little-known side of Ahmedabad.

Ahmedabad as a Centre of Learning and Education
Within a century of the foundation of Ahmedabad as the new capital of the Gujarat Sultanate, the city became a seat of Arabic and Persian learning and education. The process began with Sultan Ahmed Shah himself. His grandfather Zafar Khan, who established the Gujarat Sultanate, was based in Patan, which had been the capital of the Gujarat kingdom since the 10th century. Even at that time, Gujarat's prosperity attracted Chishti saints; we find references to an 11th-century madrasa in Patan making it perhaps the oldest centre of Islamic learning in Gujarat. Zafar Khan (Muzaffar Shah I) ensured that his grandson was educated by Patan's best teachers. Later, Ahmed Shah was accomplished enough to compose Persian couplets and, as sultan, became a patron of scholars and saints.

This process was taken forward by Ahmed Shah's grandson, Sultan Mahmud Begada, who established a Bureau of Translation which translated Arabic books into Persian. Notable translations in this phase were Yusuf bin Ahmad bin Muhammad bin Uthman's Persian rendition of the voluminous biographical dictionary of Ibn Khallikan in 1487 and Ibn Afrash's translation of *Kitab-ash Shifa*, a biography of the Prophet. Ahmedabad experienced a tremendous expansion during Mahmud Begada's rule. He invited merchants, artisans, and craftspeople to settle in the city and among these were paper manufacturers, bookbinders, and calligraphers who played a significant role in the production of books. Begada also had a Sanskrit court poet, Udayraj, who composed a panegyric to Begada entitled *Rajvinod*. Mahmud Begada's son Muzaffar Shah II was the most accomplished of

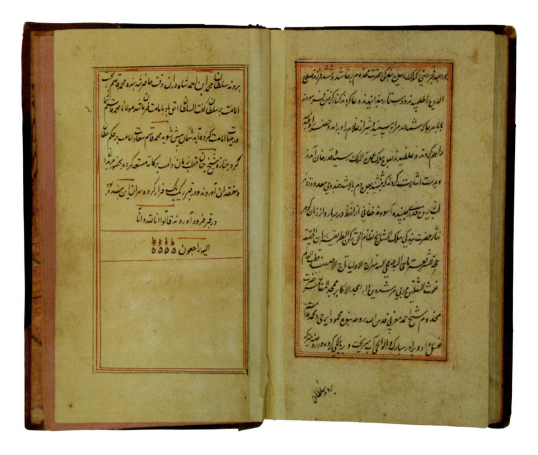

1

Tohfatul Majalis, biographical details about the pious life of Sheikh Ahmed Khattu, 17th century.

all the Gujarat Sultans – a scholar, poet, calligraphist, musician, and carpenter. He was the last of the sultans to encourage learning and scholarship.

Gujarat grew in prosperity and political stability under these three sultans and before long scholars, Sufis, and saints were drawn to Ahmedabad. Most of them came from Rajasthan, Punjab, Sind, and areas further west such as Persia, Yemen, and Egypt. They settled down in the city under the patronage of the sultans and their nobles. During this period, independent Muslim sultanates rose to power in the Deccan – the Barid Shahi dynasty at Bidar, Adil Shahi at Bijapur, Nizam Shahi at Ahmednagar, Qutb Shahi at Golconda, and Imad Shahi at Berar. These sultanates too attracted scholars and saints, and as Ahmedabad lay midway on the land route from the north to the Deccan, many of these men of learning stopped at the city. Some halted here on their way to Mecca through the port of Cambay (Khambhat), 60 kilometres from Ahmedabad. Eventually, many scholars, saints, and poets made the city their home. One of these was Hazrat Pir Muhammad Shah, a Bijapur-born Sufi saint who came to Ahmedabad in the late 17th century and whose disciples laid the foundations of the library described in this essay.

After Muzaffar II, the Gujarat Sultanate entered a period of decline till it was finally annexed to the Mughal empire by Akbar in 1573. The production of books continued in the Mughal period, and madrasas and libraries continued to flourish in the city under the patronage of the emperors. Akbar's first court poet Ghazali Mashhadi visited Ahmedabad, and lies buried in the mausoleum complex of Sheikh Ahmed Khattu (a Maghribi Sufi saint who was Sultan Ahmed Shah's contemporary, with whose blessings Ahmedabad was established, figure 1). Many poets visited the city during the reigns of Jahangir and Shahjahan and some made their home here. Mughal governors who administered the province also extended patronage to scholars and poets and had their own personal libraries. Abdur Rahim Khan-i-Khanan, who governed Gujarat under Akbar, was patron to the eminent Persian poet Naziri Nishapuri. Naziri died in Ahmedabad in 1614.

Madrasas and Libraries

Between the 15th and 18th centuries, scholars and saints started their madrasas or schools in Ahmedabad and as many of them came with their books, a library or *qutubkhana* was established with each madrasa. By the 15th–16th centuries, the *nisab* or course which was taught at a madrasa included two types of studies – *makulat*, which included philosophy, logic, the science of reading, and history; and *mankulat* which covered study of the Quran and Hadith. Teaching materials were needed at madrasas, and books began to be written to teach these subjects. Often the *ustad* or teacher made his students copy books as part of the pedagogy. The Quran and other important books such as commentaries on the Quran and Hadith were also copied by professional scribes. Some were made as gifts for the sultan and recopied when his nobles wanted copies of their own. Soon libraries of such books came into existence all over Gujarat – in Patan in the north, in Surat, Bharuch, Amod, and Ankleshwar in southern Gujarat, and in Mangrol and Kutiyana in the Kathiawad region of western Gujarat.

Six great libraries came into existence at Ahmedabad and its outskirts. The oldest of these was established in the early 15th century at Sarkhej by Sheikh Ahmed Khattu. The madrasa no longer exists but some of Sheikh Ahmed Khattu's books are preserved in his mausoleum complex. Established in the late 15th century at Rasulabad was the madrasa and library of Shah Alam, a Bukhari Saiyad saint who was a contemporary of Mahmud Begada in the early part of his reign. Also established around the same time was the madrasa of Sheikh Uthman west of the Sabarmati river. There are no traces of either of these madrasas though the *takht* or seat on which Shah Alam sat while he taught can still be seen in his mausoleum complex. Books belonging to both are in the possession of their

2
Anwarul Tanzil, treatise by Wajihuddin Alawi, early 17th century.

ARABIC-PERSIAN SCHOLARSHIP

spiritual successors. Among these is the *Jumat-i-Shahiya*, a six-volume collection of Shah Alam's Friday lectures, and *Rozat-i-Shahiya*, his lectures on Sufism in 24 volumes.

In the Khanpur area of the walled core of Ahmedabad was the madrasa of the 16th-century scholar Shah Wajihuddin Alawi who came to Ahmedabad from Champaner on the invitation of Muzaffar II. Wajihuddin wrote very few books himself (figure 2) but the glosses and notes made by him indicate that he had a vast collection of books in his library. Some of these are now in the library of the B.J. Institute of Learning and Research at Ahmedabad. The establishment of madrasas and libraries continued after the coming of the Mughals. Prominent in this period was the late-17th-century Madrasa-i-Hidayat Baksh presided over by Maulana Nuruddin. Located within the precincts of the official residence of the *qazi* or judge of Ahmedabad, the rooms of the madrasa were extant till a few decades ago and books from this library are said to be in the custody of the *qazi*'s descendants. Equally well known was the madrasa of Hasan Muhammad Chishti located in Shahibag; its collection of books is in the custody of his present *sajjada nashin* (spiritual descendant).

Arabic and Persian Inscriptions
Another glimpse of Ahmedabad's pre-eminent place in Arabic and Persian scholarship is offered by inscriptions in the city's many monuments from the medieval period onwards. These are carved in wood, sandstone, and marble in mosques and mausoleums, on stepwells, city walls, and graves. They provide valuable information about the history of their time, descriptions of the circumstances and settings in which the monuments were built, and the patrons who supported their construction. The oldest one is dated 1035 CE, and is one of the earliest inscriptions commemorating the construction of a mosque in India. Inscriptions continue to appear till the late 18th century, and scholars such as M.A. Chaghatai estimate this to be by far the longest period covered by inscriptions among all the historical cities of India. A few Sanskrit inscriptions in the Nagari script are seen in stepwells.

Most of the available inscriptions are written in fine Naskh, Nastaliq, and Tughra styles of calligraphy in a particularly decorative form. The refined and elegant forms point to the high level of craftsmanship available in the city. In two locations, the names of the calligraphists are also mentioned: an inscription at the Shams Khan Masjid built near the Shahpur area in 1539 mentions the calligraphist Abdul Hay, son of Ali, and the mosque of Sheikh Hasan Chishti built in 1565 in the same locality has a Nastaliq inscription mentioning Dost Muhammad Shukar as its creator.

The text of the inscriptions indicates the high level of accomplishment in the Arabic and Persian languages in the city. In many of the inscriptions, lines of poetry accompany the factual details about the building and these compositions point to the fact that the city had many talented poets. Most of them are anonymous though we find several mentions of one called Yahya in the 1530s.

The Collection at Hazrat Pir Muhammad Shah Dargah Sharif Library
Hazrat Pir Muhammad Shah was born in Bijapur in 1686. Having lost his father before birth, he was brought up by his uncle Hazrat Abdur Rehman who educated him at home. By the age of seven, the young Muhammad Shah could recite the Quran from memory and, recognizing his gifts, Abdur Rehman sent him to Medina and Mecca for further studies. Muhammad Shah was drawn to *tasawuf* or mysticism and on his return to Ahmedabad after some 13 years, he became renowned as a pious, saintly figure of the Qadiri Shattari Sufi order. He died in 1750 and his disciples, mostly from the Sunni Bohra community of Ahmedabad and Kadi (on the northern periphery of Ahmedabad), later established the dargah and library existing today.

The library started as a traditional *qutubkhana* with books that Pir Muhammad Shah had brought with him from Arabia. Later, disciples gave their personal collections of books written in Gujarat and other parts of India as well as books they had brought from their travel to important centres of Islamic scholarship such as Mecca, Medina, Damascus, Kufa, Cairo, Istanbul, and from Morocco, Iran, and areas northwest of India. These manuscripts were stored in *sanduq*s or wooden boxes till the present library building was constructed in 1920. Today, located a short way off from the Jami Masjid in Ahmedabad, the library has about 4,000 unique, rare, and important manuscripts and books in Arabic, Persian, and Gujari along with inscriptions in stone and, more rarely seen, in wood. The collection reflects the intellectual climate of Gujarat, and the city of Ahmedabad, between the 15th and 18th centuries.

Significant Manuscripts

The library has an extensive collection of manuscripts which point to Gujarat's place in Sufi thought and scholarship and the contribution of the saints of Ahmedabad. Among these are Sheikh Ahmed Khattu's *Al-Faraiz-ul-Ahmadiya* on Islamic jurisprudence dedicated to Sultan Ahmed Shah and *Shah-i-Risala-i-Ahmadiya* which gives information of the saints of the Maghribi Sufi order to which he belonged; Suhrawardy saint Burhanuddin Qutb-i-Alam's *Musilut-Talibin* and *Al-Musililallah* by his son Shah Alam, who was a revered saint in the 15th century and guardian of Sultan Mahmud Begada. Pir Muhammad Shah also wrote a number of treatises in Persian which were collected as *Nur-us Shuyukh* and *Ishqullah* in Gujari, a form of proto-Urdu which developed in Gujarat in the late Sultanate period. There are also manuscripts providing information on other Sufi orders in Ahmedabad and their prominent saints (figure 3).

Another important category of manuscripts covers various aspects of Islamic scholarship. There are several copies of the Quran from the 13th to the 17th centuries with fine calligraphy and decorated with floral motifs (figures 4–7). In some of these the meaning of the Arabic passages is rendered alongside in Persian in ink of a contrasting colour. The library also has probably the oldest Persian translation of the Quran in India done at Batwa (Vatva), a suburb of Ahmedabad in the late 15th century (figure 4). Unfortunately, only the second half of this manuscript is available. Two exquisite scrolls of unknown provenance and age render the Quran and blessings in *khat-i-ghubar* or dust calligraphy (figure 8) where the Arabic letters are so fine as to be practically invisible to the naked eye.

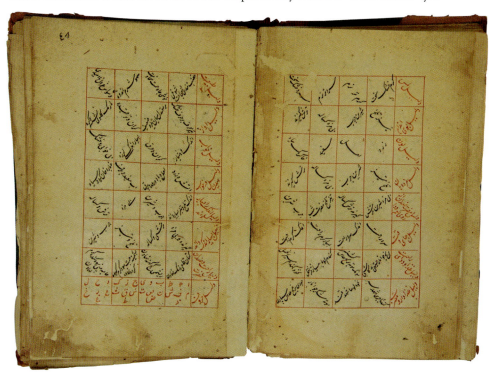

3
Hifz-e Maratib, describing Sufi spiritualism, written in Ahmedabad, 16th century.

4
The oldest Persian translation of the Quran in India, late 15th century.

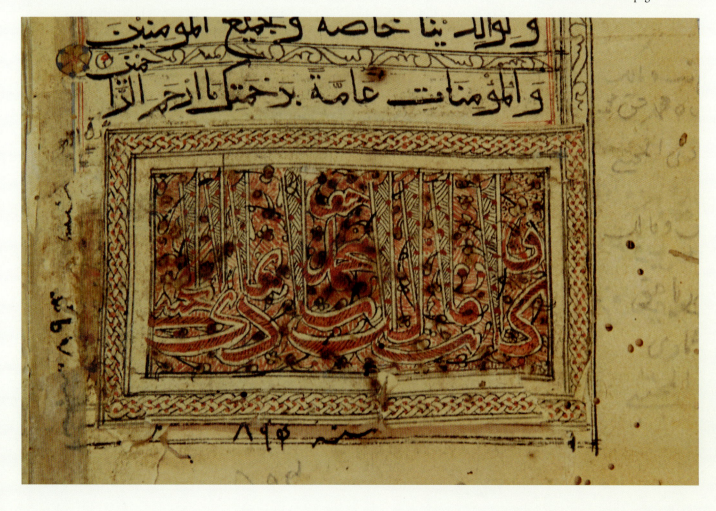

4a
Detail of the oldest Persian Quran, showing the date of its completion at the bottom of the page.

5
Calligraphy in a 16th-century Quran.

6 (below)
Calligraphy in a 16th-century Quran.

7 (below right)
Miniature full edition of handwritten Quran, late 19th–early 20th century.

Arabic-Persian Scholarship | 57

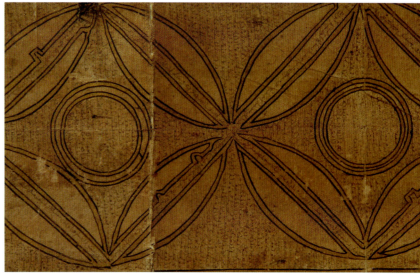

8a and b
Details of Quran scroll in *khat-i-ghubar* dust calligraphy. The calligraphy is in the grey parts.

There are works on allied religious sciences like *qirat* and *tajwid* (recitation of the Quran), *tafsir* (Quranic exegesis), *hadith* and *usul-i-hadith* (tradition and principles of tradition), *fiqh* and *usul-i-fiqh* (jurisprudence and principles of jurisprudence), and *tasawuf* (mysticism). The important and unique manuscripts at the library in this category are *Majma-ul Bihar-ul Anwar* on Hadith by Maulana Muhammad bin Tahir Pattani, a renowned 16th-century traditionalist (figure 9), and his other composition *Asma-ur Rijal* on the Prophet's companions and followers. There are commentaries on the Quran such as *Tafsir-i-Rehmani* by the 15th-century scholar Makhdoom Ali Mahaimi, and many copies of the *Badiut Tafsir* commentary including a unique copy by the 17th-century Arabic scholar Mohammad Siddique. The library has works of eminent savants and teachers like the 17th-century Maulana Ahmad bin Sulaiman Kurd's *Tasawuuf Manba-ul-Khairat* with the author's autograph. A copy of *Sharhah Shatibi* on the correct recitation of the Quran bears the seal of Sultan Ahmed Shah (figure 10).

Through the seals, colophons, ownership notes, and chronogrammatic fragments on many manuscripts in the library's collection we learn that they were part of royal libraries (for example the copy of *Mirsad-ul-Ibad*, a Persian work of the 13th century, which belonged to the libraries of emperors Shahjahan and Aurangzeb; and a copy of *Kashful-Mahjub* that bears the seal of Mughal empress Nur Jahan) or belonged to saints, scholars, nobles, officials of the administration, traders, and even ordinary readers including non-Muslims. Combined with the information we have about the madrasas of the time, we can conclude that Arabic and Persian scholarship was widespread in a significant section of society. Mention of Lahore, Ahmedabad and other cities of Gujarat, and Nauraspur – the capital of the Adil Shahis – indicates that these books circulated in Ahmedabad and Gujarat and also among the larger pan-Indian Muslim community.

In addition to books on Islamic subjects, the library has two Persian translations of the *Mahabharata*. The first is a translation of chapter 14 made by Jivandas Vadnagari in 1483 (figure 11), and the second is by Abul Fazl, Akbar's historian. Another interesting manuscript is of Radha-Krishna *pad* (verses) in Persian, Gujari, and in the Devanagari script. A prized possession is a copy of *Ghurrat-ul-Zijat*, Al Biruni's Arabic translation of *Karnatilaka*, a Sanskrit treatise on astronomy by Pandit Baijnath of Allahabad (figure 12).

Apart from books on religious matters, the library has many manuscripts of poetry (figure 13). There are several commentaries on the *Masnavi* of Maulana Rumi, particularly a copy of *Nuskha-i-Nasikha-Masnaviyyat-i-Saqima* by Gujarati scholar-statesman Shaikh Abdul-Latif Abbasi of Ahmedabad during Shahjahan's time. It bears the author's seal and autographed endorsement of having presented the copy to Mir Muhammad Qasim whose

58   MOHAIUDDIN BOMBAYWALA

9
Majma-ul Bihar-ul Anwar, compiled by Muhammad bin Tahir Pattani, late 16th century.

10
Folio of *Sharhah Shatibi* bearing the seal of Sultan Ahmed Shah, early 15th century.

10a
Detail of seal.

Arabic-Persian Scholarship

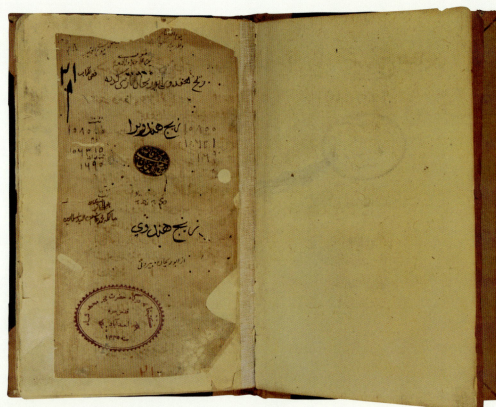

11
Mahabharata, chapter 14, a late-15th-century Persian translation by Pandit Jivandas of Vadnagar, transcribed c. 17th century.

12
Ghurrat-ul-Zijat, a 16th-century copy of Al Biruni's Arabic translation of Pandit Baijnath's *Karnatilaka*.

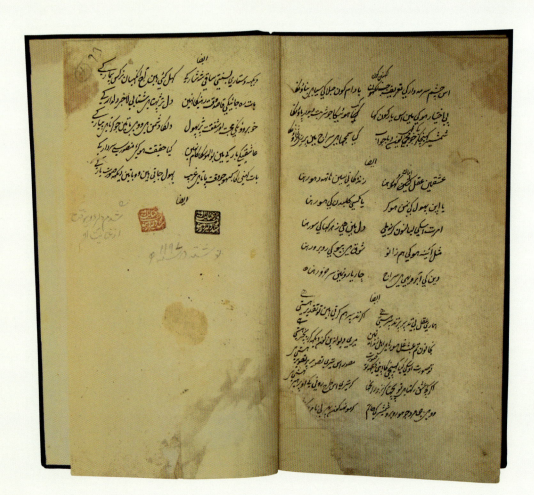

13
Gujari poems of the 17th century.

14a
Collection of ghazals by Humayun and others, early 17th century. Humayun's name is in the golden part at the top of the page.

14b
Floral decorations on another page of the same book.

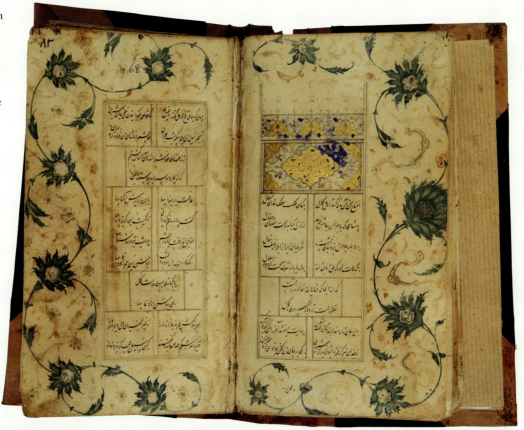

Arabic-Persian Scholarship | 61

seal is also seen. Another unique manuscript is a copy of Sa'di's *Gulistan* transcribed by the eminent Suhrawardy saint Syed Jalaluddin at the behest of Emperor Jahangir. The colophon says that it was copied from calligrapher Yaqoot al Mustasami's manuscript which was itself copied from an original autographed by Sa'di. Other volumes of poetry include a *Diwan* of Persian ghazals by Humayun and others (figure 14), *Diwan-e-Vali* by Vali Gujarati, and Al Aidrusi's *Diwani*. Interestingly, there are compositions of poetry by ordinary people such as those in praise of Pir Muhammad Shah by his followers, including his women disciples.

The library also has books on *falakiyyat* or *nujum* (astronomy, figure 15), *khattati* (calligraphy), *tib* (medicine), *itriyyat* (perfumery), *tir-andazi* (archery), *tefung-sazi* (gunnery), and *musique* (music). Also in the dargah complex are numerous stone inscriptions in fine calligraphy as well as wooden inscriptions in the library's collection in equally fine craftsmanship (figures 16 and 17).

The collection is important from different points of view, furnishing as it does sufficient and unutilized material for understanding the contribution of India in general, and Gujarat and Ahmedabad in particular, to Persian, Arabic, and Urdu literature in the fields of the traditional as well as intellectual sciences. It also throws light on the calligraphy and craft skills which facilitated this scholarship and offers a glimpse of the nature of patronage which sustained it.

Figure Acknowledgements
All photographs courtesy of the Hazrat Pir Muhammad Shah Dargah Sharif Library, Ahmedabad. Photographers: Kunal Panchal and Narendra Raghunath.

Further Reading
Abdullah Muhammad bin Umar, Hajji al-dabir, Sir Denison Ross (ed.), *Zafar al-Wali bi Muzaffar wal-Alih*, 3 Parts, London: John Murray, 1910–28.
Abul Fazl Allami, Col. H.S. Jarrett (trans.), *Ain-i-Akbari* Vol. 2, third edition, New Delhi: Oriental Book Reprint Corporation, 1978.
Ali Muhammad Khan, M.F. Lokhandwala (trans.), *Mirat-i-Ahmadi*, Baroda: Oriental Institute, M.S. University, 1965.

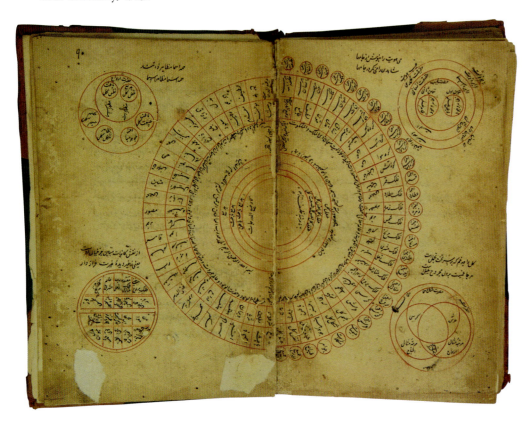

15
Page from *Hifz-e Maratib* showing cosmological charts, c. 16th century.

16
Stone inscription on Pir Muhammad Shah's dargah building, 17th century.

17
Wooden inscription, line from Hadith, c. 16th century.

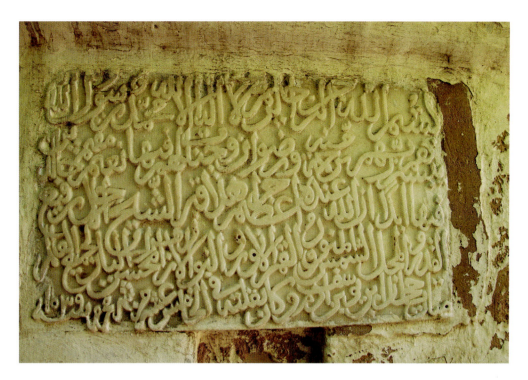

Chaghtai, M.A., *Muslim Monuments of Ahmedabad through their Inscriptions*, Poona: Bulletin of the Deccan College Research Institute, Poona, 1942.

Desai, Z.A., "The Major Dargahs of Ahmedabad" in C.W. Troll (ed.), *Muslim Shrines in India*, New Delhi: Oxford University Press, 1989.

Descriptive Catalogues of Manuscripts of the Hazrat Pir Muhammad Shah Dargah Sharif Library, Vols. 1–10, Ahmedabad, 1991–2010, introductory essays.

Husain, S.M. Azizuddin (ed.), *Madrasa Education in India: Eleventh to Twenty First Century*, New Delhi: Kanishka Publishers, 2005.

Manjhu, Sikandar, E.C. Bayley (trans.), *Mirat-i-Sikandari*, New Delhi: S. Chand and Company, 1970.

Nadvi, S.A. Zafar, "Libraries during the Muslim Rule in India", Pt. 1, *Islamic Culture* 19(4), 1945, pp. 329–47; pt. 2, *Islamic Culture* 20(1), 1946, pp. 3–20.

Quraishi, M.A., *Muslim Education and Learning of Gujarat (1297–1758)*, Vadodara: M.S. University, 1972.

Schimmel, Annemarie, *Islamic Calligraphy*, Leiden: E.J. Brill, 1970.

Sharma, Sunil, "Urdu and Persian Scholarly Publishing in Contemporary Gujarat", *The Annual of Urdu Studies* 20, 2005, pp. 296–302.

Thackston, Wheeler M., *The Jahangirnama: Memoirs of Jahangir, Emperor of India*, New York: Oxford University Press, 1999.

Incubating
Indian Modernism

Himanshu Burte

Chandigarh was chosen (and created) as a purpose-built research laboratory for introducing a full-blown modernism into 1950s India. But Ahmedabad *chose* to become the first *field* laboratory of modernism in India.[1] That distinction illuminates the unusually close relationship between modernism as a specific approach to architecture in the industrial age, and the very particular brand of local modernity that emerged in Ahmedabad in the 20th century.

This essay offers a brief and selective reading of the way the modernist attitude to architecture has developed in Ahmedabad. This is likely to be relevant for three reasons. First, Ahmedabad is perhaps unique among Indian cities in the aspirational force that architecture of modernist lineage still carries in residential, institutional, and even commercial projects among the clientele. Secondly, it is also the city that has disseminated modernist values and design skills successfully across the country through the National Institute of Design (NID) and the School of Architecture at the Centre for Environmental Planning and Technology (CEPT).[2] The School of Architecture has also shaped the way architecture is taught in many different institutions in India. The third reason is the rich social history underlying the successful grafting of the modernist shoot onto the then 550-year-old body and imagination of Ahmedabad.

Patronage for Modernism
Modernism's success (and transformation) in India owes much to the mid-20th-century civil society of Ahmedabad dominated by a few business families related to each other by ties of blood and marriage. For a while after Independence in 1947, members of these families also had a significant influence on urban politics in Ahmedabad.

Traditionally involved in trading, these families had switched to industry from the middle of the 19th century. Soon Ahmedabad became a centre of textile production and came to be called the "Manchester of the East". Through the mechanism of the mahajan – a traditional association of businessmen – members of the business community had traditionally sustained a context of cooperative action which kept competition within productive limits.[3] The broader agenda of the business community had also been affected by the two-decade-long presence of Gandhi in the city, having alternately supported and fought him in different ways – the latter most notably when he went on a hunger strike in 1918 in support of the workers' demand for survival wages. From the time he settled in Ahmedabad in 1915, and began directing the nationwide movement for social reform and independence from British rule from his ashram on the Sabarmati, Gandhi had begun injecting his value system into the emerging public sphere of the city. The business community, with its already strong tradition of contributing to and shaping public life, was not unaffected by this. Its various initiatives in civic improvement, institution-building, and cultural development during the first half of the 20th century, appear to have two characteristics. These initiatives are marked by a careful safeguarding of profitable business activity in general. At the same time they show a commitment (reflected in the time, effort, and money spent) to upgrading the social and physical infrastructure in the city, without expecting *immediate* returns. Many of these initiatives, like the setting up of the NID and Indian Institute of Management (IIM), would benefit business activity at least indirectly, or in the future. However, others, like the Indian Space Research Organisation (ISRO) that Vikram Sarabhai helped found, were perhaps approached more as a contribution to the task of incubating modernity at a national scale.

The prominent business families of the city, the Sarabhais and the Lalbhais in particular, played an important part in this development, as did Balkrishna Doshi, then a young architect just returned from Le Corbusier's studio in France to help with work at Chandigarh. Doshi was instrumental in securing millowners' support for the influential American architect, Louis Kahn, to build in Ahmedabad. He also lobbied hard, but unsuccessfully, to have Louis Kahn appointed as the architect of Gandhinagar, the new capital city created for Gujarat.[4] Further, in 1962, he coordinated the founding of CEPT and has been closely associated with it ever since.

It also helped that Ambalal Sarabhai's own son and daughter, Gautam and Gira (who had worked with Frank Lloyd Wright), were accomplished designers. Together they would design the elegant campus of the NID, one of the important, if underrated, works of early Indian modernism. Meanwhile, Kasturbhai Lalbhai supported the institution of CEPT under the Ahmedabad Education Society, a charitable trust he chaired.

The business community of Ahmedabad supported modernism in three interconnected ways. First, the industrialists sponsored invitations and provided projects for two international masters – Le Corbusier (in the 1950s) and Louis Kahn (in the 1960s) – to build in Ahmedabad, which was then a small city. Le Corbusier built four projects in the city, and Kahn, the large IIM campus.[5] Secondly, through these projects the community also ensured opportunities for young Indian architects to work with the international masters, and later provided them with projects. For instance, NID was made the architect of record for the IIM project, with Doshi overseeing the design team. Among the people in the team were Sen Kapadia, who was to become an important architect and institution-builder in Mumbai in the 1980s and '90s, as well as Sharad Shah, a structural engineer who would be based in Mumbai and collaborate with Doshi, Charles Correa, and Achyut Kanvinde on many important projects.

But the third prong of support was perhaps to prove most crucial for the sustenance of modernism in India. It was the support for founding the two major design institutions in the city, NID (1961) and CEPT (1962) that remain undisputed leaders in design education in India even today. These two institutions also attracted talented young architects and designers into the faculty, many of whom practised their craft in the city, thus enriching its physical and creative milieu.

The three lines of action and support also involved important synergies. For instance, the example of the international masters – whether at Ahmedabad Textile Millowner's Association (ATMA) or IIM – could be engaged and critiqued in projects that local architects produced "after the masters" as it were.[6] These works – Doshi's own office Sangath, Anant Raje's Management Development Centre at IIM, Hasmukh Patel's Newman Hall – became local examples to emulate and critique for students and younger practitioners who gathered at CEPT. In the absence of even one of these three lines of action in Ahmedabad, modernism in India would have been much poorer than it is. The Ahmedabad elite thus provided to civil society a complement to the early confidence reposed in modernism by the Nehruvian state at Chandigarh. The different levels of support also ensured that a favourable climate was created for the different transformations of modernism by architects like Doshi, Patel, Raje, and Leo Pereira in Ahmedabad from the 1960s to the 1990s.

Forms of Modernity

An important distinction between modern and modernist architecture is worth making here. Architecture built with modern methods, to suit modern programmes, using modern industrial materials like cement, steel, and reinforced cement concrete (RCC), designed by trained architects practising as modern consultants (as opposed to the traditional master-builders), and built by contractors following modern contracting arrangements already existed in Ahmedabad before the advent of modernism. Accomplished architects like Claude Batley (of Gregson, Batley and King, Bombay), Atmaram Gajjar, and Asarpota had built a number of extremely well-crafted buildings in the modern mode of architectural practice. Batley's elegant Electric House (c. 1940) and Town Hall, and Gajjar's Gujarat University (1947) are significant examples in this regard.

What distinguishes this body of work from that of the modernism that came later was its desire (largely through the Art Deco paradigm) for a sense of continuity with the immediate colonial architectural past even when the imagery was precolonial. In spite of its immediate American roots, much Art Deco architecture in India, and what is sometimes called Indo Deco, preserves fundamental compositional attributes of 19th-century European and colonial architecture (symmetry, legibility, decorative structure, etc.), even as it adopts a more abstract attitude towards detail. Art Deco as practised with different modifications in India, generally, is distinct from but not necessarily antagonistic towards either colonial architecture or its European inspiration. In fact, Indianized Art Deco tended to contrast more with the local architectural traditions it borrowed motifs from. Simply put, thus, the many varieties of Indianized Deco in practice in the city did not try to challenge or overthrow the dominant deep structure underlying colonial architecture.

Perhaps for this reason, though substantively modern in many ways and popular at a civic level till Independence, the architecture of the kind practised by Batley, Asarpota, or Gajjar faded slowly but quietly after Independence. At the same time, it appears that these *modern* architects also prepared the ground for the successful execution of the *modernist* visions to follow.[7] By the time modernists entered the scene following the example of Le Corbusier, these architects had already set up a capable culture of building with relatively modern work processes and technologies like RCC.

The fading of this approach, perhaps, offers some clues, by implication, to the specific attraction modernism, and its claims, might have had for young architects in a newly independent nation and for the Ahmedabad elite. The utopian and futurist orientation of modernism (and lack of complicated baggage of the past, or just plain denial of it), its espousal of rationality, the apparent non-elitism involved in its use of everyday industrial materials, and the sheer novelty of its expressive system proved attractive to an elite keen that the country move on.

Modernism in Ahmedabad

The modernism that arrived in Ahmedabad in the 1950s with Le Corbusier, as with Achyut Kanvinde's Ahmedabad Textile Industry's Research Association (ATIRA, 1952) and Physical Research Laboratory (PRL, 1954) projects, was largely of European pedigree.[8] European modernism was committed to universalist principles. It looked at peculiarities of place and of socio-cultural history as distractions from the task of shaping the future. Instead, modernism turned away from the past and sought to give form in advance to the coming future of what we might today call hyper-industrialization particularly in the West.

Modernism's expressive force often turned on the phenomenon of alienation.[9] The building itself was deliberately alienated from its surroundings, and preferred to confront nature as its opposite. Simultaneously, the building actively alienated the dweller in his or her attempt at taking possession of it cognitively or through the small actions of habitation. Modernist form pursued perfect geometry, emptiness (in walls and spaces), a rejection of all cultural associations except with its own physical substance. Not surprisingly, abstraction was the preferred mode of expression for modernist architects.[10]

Such was the modernism that came to India from the late 1940s through Le Corbusier and young architects like Doshi, Correa, and Kanvinde who had trained in the West. It can be characterized as anti-domestic in two senses. With some important exceptions it did

1
Ahmedabad Textile Millowners' Association (ATMA). Architect Le Corbusier. Photograph: Himanshu Burte.

2
Ahmedabad Textile
Millowners' Association
(ATMA). Architect Le
Corbusier. Photograph:
Himanshu Burte.

3
Sarabhai House. Architect
Le Corbusier. Photograph:
Rajesh Sagara.

not believe in "home", being marked by an attitude of *leaving* home behind.[11] Home was seen as the site of everyday life. Modernist architecture sought to transcend the everyday and speak compulsively on what it imagined to be a more exalted plane. It was non-domestic in the second sense, by being literally a foreign import into India which was not always open to accommodating local habitational values.

Le Corbusier (and Louis Kahn to some extent) offered the template for emulating European modernism in different ways. At the same time, however, their work also contained the seeds of the very critique that Ahmedabad architects would develop from the 1970s in their buildings. Three of Le Corbusier's projects in Ahmedabad – ATMA, Shodhan House, and Sanskar Kendra – exemplify a clearly modernist attitude as described above (figures 1 and 2). But his fourth, Sarabhai House, is in many ways their opposite (figure 3).[12] It is much more deeply entangled in its setting, works like a frame for experiencing the garden, encourages you to forget it in the pleasure of dwelling, and is self-effacing as a form. In spite of the many alienating challenges it offered for everyday family life (no doors!), it can be seen as the valuable counterpoint, within the modernist tradition, to his other three buildings.

In Kahn's case, such contradictory impulses are brought into balance in the single project he built in India, the IIMA (figures 4 and 5). The monumental campus for this very modern and future-oriented institution echoes ruins from the past. Through the ancient building material, brick, as well as through a very traditional pursuit of darkness he also connects the modern building to its location. The fort-like scale and the unrelenting rhythms of overscaled elements alienate, but just enough for the dweller to attend consciously to the buildings intermittently, while transiting from one relatively intimate space to another.

4
Indian Institute of Management, Ahmedabad (IIMA). Architect Louis Kahn. Photograph: Himanshu Burte.

5
Interior view of IIMA. Architect Louis Kahn. Photograph: Himanshu Burte.

After an initial phase of emulating Corbusian or functionalist modernism, by the mid-1970s Indian and Ahmedabadi modernism had developed a diverse set of approaches which shared one common value (which was never articulated in these terms): a commitment to the idea of place.[13] The shared orientation was towards a more communicative and habitable avatar of modernism (figure 6). It also affirmed that place mattered. Place as a value can refer to a sense of situatedness, as well as to the human-responsiveness of a built

INDIAN MODERNISM | 71

6
Centre for Environment Planning and Technology (CEPT). Architect Balkrishna Doshi. Photograph: Himanshu Burte.

7
Premabhai Hall. Architect Balkrishna Doshi. Photograph: Dinesh Shukla.

space. This meant that buildings would be shaped around (not against) the pressures of the natural or historic urban context, climate, and topography. It also meant that spaces would be designed to invite dwelling and to become loved places.

Of course, much before Le Corbusier was done with India or Kahn had begun building IIM, Charles Correa had already built a lasting essay in placemaking – Gandhi Smarak Sangrahalaya at Gandhi's ashram on the Sabarmati river. Even early emulation of Corbusian modernism in Ahmedabad already foreshadowed a habitational sensitivity at Doshi's L.D. Institute of Indology. A museum built in 1959–62, it is remarkably human in scale, though its form still seeks to "float" off the ground and be of no place in particular.[14] Of course, even in the 1970s there are projects like Doshi's Premabhai Hall (designed in the early 1970s and built by 1977), which confronts a lively historical urban place, Bhadra Square, with an outsized and disengaged monumental object (figure 7). But at the Indian Institute of Management, Bangalore (1977–84) Doshi revealed a transformed modernism, monumental but with a strong connection to location (through granite, the local stone) and a unique spatial character. At the same time he also built Sangath (1981), his own office in Ahmedabad, perhaps his most poetic building, answering the contrary calls of earth and sky simultaneously (figure 8).

Apart from Doshi, three other architects have been most significant in the transformation of modernism in Ahmedabad: Hasmukh Patel, Anant Raje, and Leo Pereira. All of them modified and consolidated modernism in different ways through teaching and practice. Patel, who bought over the practice of Atmaram Gajjar as a young man, fostered a culture of efficient, elegant, and durable building through what is now a large practice (now managed by his son Bimal, an architect and urban planner) active in the commercial and governmental sector. He connected and consolidated values of good

8
Sangath. Architect Balkrishna Doshi. Photograph courtesy Sangath.

architectural craftsmanship that were at the centre of modernism as well as of Ahmedabad's distinguished architectural tradition. In his institutional and residential projects (especially his own home), he also achieved a sensitive modulation of scale that remains a core value in Indian modernism.

But it is perhaps Leo Pereira who is most closely identified in Ahmedabad with the idea of intimate and engaging scales in architecture. Pereira worked with Patel for seven years before setting up his own small practice. Like Raje, he has built less in Ahmedabad than in other cities in Gujarat, like Bhavnagar. Pereira's work addresses issues of place and dwelling through miniaturization. That strategy creates a comfortable body-hugging space and form, and minimizes heat gain as well as material consumption. His own house closes against the harsh summer till only a glowing darkness pervades in the interior. Its internal scales are also modulated skilfully so that the intimacy of low ceilings at places (window lintels at a height of approximately 1.5 metres), makes ordinary 3-metre room heights elsewhere appear expansive. Pereira has consistently transferred the insight and skill underlying such design achievement to the design studio at the School of Architecture.

Something similar can be said about Raje's influence. Raje is widely regarded as an architect's architect in India. Respectfully treating Kahn's example as a starting point – he worked with Kahn in his Philadelphia office for a few years and then had his own office in the IIM campus for many years – Raje developed his own expressive range. He was most successful among Indian architects of his generation in imbuing modernist form with a directly representational content. His special skill, most evident at the Indian Institute of Forest Management (IIFM), Bhopal, lay in ushering echoes from the past into convincingly contemporary spaces and forms.

Critiques of Indian Modernism
There is an absence of a strong critical culture in Indian architecture. Critiques of the transformation of modernism by architects like Doshi, Pereira, and Raje that have emerged since the 1980s have thus been best expressed in built work especially from the 1990s. Rarely formulated systematically in published form by practising architects or academics, critical positions must often be read off built form.

One line of criticism appears to question the value of the transformation of modernism by architects like Doshi, Raje, and Patel. Different positions and value priorities appear to intersect in this critique, best expressed in the most celebrated work of Gurjeet Singh Matharoo (b. 1966) and Bimal Patel (b. 1960). Both architects received undergraduate training in CEPT. Both work extensively in exposed concrete. Both are die-hard minimalists, though early in their career both produced buildings that are much more "decorative" in comparison.[15] Both like to craft buildings as formally self-sufficient objects that are results of pouring material down, not building it up. Both have stripped off even the least representational of elements from the visible "crust" of Indian modernist architecture that was their inheritance. Beyond that they differ significantly in approach. Matharoo is much more intensive in his sculptural and spatial modulation following the example of Le Corbusier in India.[16] His designs for Prathama (a blood bank), a crematorium in Surat, and some houses testify to this. Patel, meanwhile reaches for an approach that seeks the existential depth achieved by Louis Kahn and the systemic rigour of Mies van der Rohe.[17] His most ambitious architectural project, an extension campus for IIM across the road from Kahn's masterly essay in brick and shadow, reveals his twin debts. It is also reflected in the mammoth Sabarmati Redevelopment Project he has designed.

Other architects too participate in this return to a purer abstraction. Underlying this commitment is an impatience with what are seen as untenable excesses of discourse and design accompanying the transformation of modernism from the 1970s. In pursuit of

9
Sabarmati Riverfront view.
Architect Bimal Patel.
Photograph: Himanshu Burte.

strategies for localization, architects like Doshi, Correa, and Raj Rewal often sought out myths, images, and motifs from the past as heuristic aids for design or communicational devices. Their connection with the essential architectural programme of individual projects could be ambiguous and they were sometimes accused of exoticization. Architects of Matharoo and Patel's generation have reacted by rejecting the entire expressive paradigm of Indian modernism – and not only its problematic aspects. They appear to have returned directly to the "purer" modernism of European origin for inspiration.

Furthermore I believe that this choice is also related to the global re-emergence of modernist grammar (sans the progressive or avant-garde ideology of early modernism) as *the* legitimate mode for serious architecture. While this grammar has also been appropriated occasionally by commercial architecture (represented in Ahmedabad by the often skilful, but also mannerist and eclectic modernism of Apurva Amin), it has also been presented globally as being critical of a culture of consumption. What is not always acknowledged is that this minimalist grammar is simultaneously a mode of legitimizing wealth and consumption because of its sophistication. By contrast, the appeal of modernist ideology when it first came to India lay in its apparently egalitarian thrust. The monumentality of architecture at ATMA and IIM turned on the *expressed* humbleness of concrete and brick.

What complicates the return to a purer modernism is the fact that, unlike Indian modernism after the 1970s, it does not seem to engage with legitimate and established criticism of the general "unfriendliness" of modernist architecture. Put another way, it represents a return to modernist "space", from the localized "place" of Indian modernism. From the street, Matharoo's Prathama is as daunting to the visitor (though it has moments of great experiential depth inside) as any high modernist building of the mid-20th century. Patel's severely elegant IIM extension (involved, occasionally, in a viable conversation with its classic neighbour across the street) and the sample stretch of the Sabarmati Riverfront (figure 9) promise to resist occupation and appropriation as resolutely.

A Greater Transformation
In contrast to the above, two other critiques appear to suggest that the transformation of modernism must actually go much further. Both connect in the belief that even the transformed and localized modernism-as-usual does not offer a sustainable model for architecture, socially or ecologically. One rejects the methods, materials, and aesthetic of modernism almost completely, while the other seeks to release the untapped potential for

10
Lime work exterior of Jaai and Surya Kakani residence. Architect Surya Kakani. Photograph: Himanshu Burte.

11
Interior of Jaai and Surya Kakani residence. Architect Surya Kakani. Photograph: Himanshu Burte.

sustainable approaches that has always existed deep within the modernist promise. Each of these positions is exemplified by one practice, but neither has too many fellow travellers in the city. That last fact, perhaps, points to an important limitation of contemporary architecture in Ahmedabad: a lack of significant challenges to modernism as an ideology or expressive paradigm, and a related absence of ideological diversity within the culture of socially responsible architecture in the city.[18]

Abhikram (a medium-sized practice established in 1979 by a CEPT-educated couple, Parul Zaveri and Nimish Patel) epitomizes a direct challenge to the entire modernist system of beliefs and conventions.[19] Always respectful of the wisdom, sustainability, and livability of traditional architecture, Zaveri and Patel pursue a number of interrelated agendas in projects ranging from five-star resorts and pharmaceutical labs, to individual residences. Reducing energy consumption, providing respect and livelihoods to traditional craftspeople in the building process, and conservation of built heritage are among their objectives. Their research laboratory building for Torrent Pharmaceuticals in Ahmedabad is a globally significant example of use of a passive downdraught ventilation system that has saved enormous amounts of fossil energy by replacing a conventional air-conditioning system, and provided better air quality to the laboratories.[20] Udaivilas Palace in Udaipur, meanwhile, is a modern five-star resort but built with materials (stone and lime particularly), processes, skills, and an aesthetic drawn from the past and involving traditional craftspeople. At the aesthetic level, Abhikram's work does sometimes slide towards kitsch. Negotiating the contrary pulls of modern programmes and materials on the one hand, and traditional aesthetic values on the other, is part of the challenge they have to fully master. However, Patel and Zaveri have asked difficult questions of modernism and built robust answers which must count as an important contribution.

Surya Kakani (b. 1963), who established his practice in 1995 in partnership with his graphic designer wife Jaai Kakani, has followed a different track (figures 10 and 11). His work shows how core values underlying modernism can lead to a technically rigorous, ecologically benign, and also highly livable architecture.[21] Kakani has built elegantly and well in a range of recycled and low-energy materials – flyash bricks, construction debris, thatch, bamboo. He does not reject RCC, but prefers to use load-bearing or composite construction to reduce energy consumed by steel or cement. His garment factory for Madhu Industries Limited in Ahmedabad is a composite structure with the three-storey external wall in a load-bearing combination of flyash and burnt brick (15 flyash to 1 burnt brick). The building employs an engineered passive downdraught evaporative cooling (PDEC) system (designed by Chaman Lal Gupta) for temperature and dust control instead of air-conditioning. The crenellations in the external wall enclose channels for breeze caught at the roof to be led down into every floor and conveyed out and up through the central courtyard.

At one level, Kakani's work leads us to distinguish between values and conventions in architecture, especially in modernism. He holds firmly to hoary modernist values of functional rigour, efficiency (including waste control and recycling), and minimal consumption of energy. But, from within the modernist paradigm he continually questions its formal conventions (for instance, the conventional white painted or exposed RCC forms, cantilevered masses, large glazed openings) against these core values, and also against his own core commitment to an agenda of sustainability and social equity. The intensity of that interrogation is often revealed in the unintentional severity of some of his work.

Interestingly, Kakani and Abhikram's critical and creative response to an inherited modernism has been supported by their business-minded clientele in Ahmedabad (but also outside) for its practical value. In keeping with Ahmedabad's history of innovation in business, manufacturing, and the social sector, their clients have been willing to take risks in the hope of producing more efficient, sustainable, and contextually responsive buildings. They are not part of the business families that ushered modernism into Ahmedabad in the 1950s. And they are more partners than patrons in the building process, standing to lose or benefit significantly from the material outcome. But their role is not any less important at a time when contemporary architecture in India is searching once again for truly progressive directions.

Acknowledgements

I have learnt much about Ahmedabad's modern architecture from discussions with too many people to list here, but especially Balkrishna Doshi, Miki and Madhavi Desai, Neelkanth Chhaya, Bimal Patel, Hasmukh Patel, Gurjeet Singh Matharoo, and Surya Kakani. Some of the field research in Ahmedabad related to this article was conducted as part of two separate research projects supported respectively by grants from the India Foundation for the Arts, Bangalore and the Graham Foundation for the Study of Fine Arts, Chicago. I am grateful for their support.

Notes

1 There are many modernisms, but I shall use the singular for convenience and brevity here and point out the significant internal divergences where appropriate.

2. For instance, many of the leading architects and designers of Bangalore (now Bengaluru), which is fast emerging as a centre for design excellence in India, have been educated at either of these institutions.
3. Achyut Yagnik and Suchitra Sheth, *The Shaping of Modern Gujarat: Plurality, Hindutva and Beyond*, New Delhi: Penguin Books, 2005, pp. 26–30.
4. For the fascinating history of this attempt involving many players, see Ravi Kalia, *Gandhinagar: Building National Identity in Postcolonial India*, New Delhi: Oxford University Press, 2005.
5. Le Corbusier built the Sarabhai and Shodhan Houses, the Sanskar Kendra (a museum of the city), and the ATMA building (popularly known as the Millowners' Association building).
6. Vikram Bhatt and Peter Scriver, *Contemporary Indian Architecture: After the Masters*, Ahmedabad: Mapin Publishing, 1990.
7. I am grateful to Miki Desai for pointing this out.
8. Kanvinde trained in 1945–47 at Harvard University under a German emigre and the founder of the Bauhaus, Walter Gropius, who headed the architecture programme. See Jon Lang, Madhavi Desai, and Miki Desai, *Architecture and Independence: The Search for Identity – India 1880–1980*, New Delhi: Oxford University Press, 1997, pp. 208–09, 211.
9. Brian O'Doherty, *Inside the White Cube: The Ideology of Gallery Space*, Santa Monica and San Francisco: Lapis Press, 1986, p. 73.
10. For an extended critique of modernism along these lines see Himanshu Burte, *Space for Engagement: The Indian Artplace and a Habitational Approach to Architecture*, Kolkata: Seagull Books, 2008.
11. Christopher Reed, ed., *Not at Home: The Suppression of Domesticity in Modern Art and Architecture*, London: Thames and Hudson, 1996.
12. It taps into a vein of work earlier revealed in the Erruziris house in Peru as well as in Le Corbusier's own vacation house in France, which steered the brutalist fascination with rough materials like brick towards a more place-hugging orientation.
13. For a broader discussion on the concept of place see Yi Fu Tuan's *Space and Place: The Perspective of Experience*, Minneapolis: University of Minnesota Press, 1977 and Burte 2008.
14. The plinth of Gandhi Smarak Sangrahalaya also "floats", and a very subtle Japanese influence pervades the design in general.
15. Bimal Patel's Entrepreneurship Development Institute on the outskirts of Ahmedabad won the prestigious Aga Khan Award in 1992. The exposed brick-and-concrete-arch design references colonial and precolonial forms and contrasts with Patel's current work. A school designed by Matharoo in Ajmer early in his career, too, has a surprisingly Indian modernist (or even postmodernist) exploration of arched forms as well as surface ornament.
16. The often poetic modulation of scale in Matharoo's work harks back to the slightly more sensually engaging work of Pereira.
17. The partly Miesian commitment to systemic rigour is perhaps related to the large scale of operation that Patel has inherited from his father Hasmukh. Matharoo's is a boutique studio practice, in comparison.
18. Bangalore, by contrast, has a significant diversity of approaches. Interestingly, many of the leading young architects there are educated in Ahmedabad, including those directly antithetical to modernism like Chitra Vishwanath. An important fact related to this lack of diversity is perhaps the fact that Ahmedabad has only one School of Architecture. Pune, a city of comparable size, has ten.
19. Except for the principles of rationality and efficiency, which continue to be respected outside of formal modernist conventions.
20. The cost saving was not insignificant either. The savings on the air-conditioning are estimated to have covered the entire cost of the building itself in 13 years. The passive downdraught ventilation system was designed by Short Ford Associates, London.
21. Himanshu Parikh, a renowned structural engineer, has collaborated on Kakani's projects and helped reduce consumption of energy-intensive steel and cement, by employing load-bearing and composite construction systems.

An Awakening of Modern Art

Sharmila Sagara

The late 19th century was a period of cultural transformation in Ahmedabad where the primary tools of reform were literature and poetry. Art remained in the shadow of the pen; therefore, rather than tracing a resurgence of art in post-Independence Ahmedabad, one may say that the visual arts had to begin from the beginning.[1] As with the city's architecture and crafts, modernism in art developed not only through the efforts of its citizens but also through the contributions of individuals who visited the city. Yet, art in Ahmedabad has remained within the private domain of its visionary citizens and has hardly found its way into the public realm or into its many great institutions. Thus, art may be one important facet of the profile of this city of great institutions, but it has not quite become a philosophy of Ahmedabad's being.

Art Education in Ahmedabad: The Beginnings
To understand the present art scene in Ahmedabad, it is fundamental to span the scene from the early 20th century till today, beginning with one individual – Ravishankar Raval. Ravishankar was born in 1892 in Bhavnagar. After studying painting and art history at the Sir J.J. School of Art in Bombay (Mumbai), he moved to Ahmedabad in 1919 to start a career as a creative painter, journalist, and illustrator. Ahmedabad was then a city of poets and writers who felt the lack of artists to paint posters for their literary summits and illustrate their books. It was at this time that the great poet Nanalal Dalpatram had penned the famous poem *Gujarat no Tapasvi* to mark Gandhiji's 50th birthday. The publishers needed a fresh image of Gandhiji to illustrate the poem. Declining to be photographed, Gandhiji agreed to sit for a sketch and young Ravishankar Raval was called for this job. This was an opportunity for Ravishankar to observe the great man whose immense simplicity touched his young mind and remained with him for the rest of his life. Ravishankar decided to follow Gandhiji's path and to devote his life to teaching.[2] He started Chitra Varga (art classes) for students at Gujarat Vidyapith as well as his own art classes Kala Varga, established *Kumar* – a monthly magazine carrying essays on art, literature, and politics. Ravishankar's work for the magazine was inspired by individuals and events and thus consisted of a body of portraits of people, depiction of mythological stories, and representations of political events. One of his well known works is the depiction of the famous trial of Gandhiji which took place in Ahmedabad in 1922.

A teacher by nature, Ravishankar travelled to study institutions like Tagore's Santiniketan and the Government College of Fine Arts, Madras (Chennai), and bring their various styles and techniques of teaching to Chitra Varga. His students included the industrialist Ambalal Sarabhai and members of his family including wife Sarlaben, and Sir Chinubhai Baronet and his family. Ravishankar travelled with these families to summer destinations where he shared creative space with literary artists and philosophers with whom he had the opportunity to discuss European art practices, thus instilling in him an interest in world art.[3] His students who went to different art schools to study further also brought back different traditions and styles of painting to Chitra Varga. Kanu Desai went to Santiniketan and started painting in watercolours which became a popular medium that inspired many young students. Rasiklal Parikh went to the J.J. School of Art and on his return went on to establish the Sheth C.N. College of Fine Arts at Ahmedabad in 1950.

Modernism in Art

If Ravishankar Raval was the father figure of contemporary art in Ahmedabad, it was his student Chhaganlal Jadav who introduced the language of modernism here. The painter Kanu Desai noticed this quiet boy who stood in a corner and watched Ravishankar Raval at work. Recognizing his interest and talent, Kanu Desai encouraged Chhaganlal to join Chitra Varga.

Born in Ahmedabad in 1903 in a low-caste weaver's family (a caste considered "untouchable" in Gujarat), Chhaganlal Jadav (figure 1) attended night classes at Gujarat Vidyapith where he later became a teacher. He was attracted by the watercolour silhouettes of Kanu Desai and so began his studies in painting under him. During this time Chitra Varga and Kala Varga were closed as the freedom movement engrossed the city. Chhaganlal had to spend three months in jail for participating in Gandhiji's civil disobedience movement in 1930. Thereafter he went to Indore for higher studies where he met the great painter N.S. Bendre, the master of impressionistic landscapes and portraits. Chhaganlal Jadav's friendship with Bendre inspired him as well as helped to resolve his quest for a medium of expression within painting. His early landscapes in semi-classical style were compared with those of the great master J.M.W. Turner by the then Principal of Lucknow Art College, Mr Romans.[4] Chhaganlal soon rejected this style of painting and turned to explorations of lines, forms which according to Bendre, "carry cosmic presence. His doodle-like forms explore possibility of unity as well signify intense feelings."[5] He also travelled with Bendre to the villages of India to paint life there. It was during several trips to such places and particularly to the Himalaya, that he painted the magnificence of nature, the snow peaks of mountains that expressed the aspirations of humanity and spirituality. These experiences drew Chhaganlal towards a philosophical approach to life, leading to a definite turn to abstraction. Yet, his abstraction was not in the sense of Western abstract art but carried symbols as expression of the realization of a higher entity by the artist (figure 2).

Chhaganlal's appreciation of European art and his interest in literature made an impact on young minds. The young Piraji Sagara, Mansing Chhara, Bhanu Shah, Balkrishna Patel, Haku Shah, Gajendra Shah, Ramnik Bhavsar, and Rashmi Khatri became members of the Progressive Artists Group founded in Bombay. The group was very active during the 1960s as these young artists met regularly at a city restaurant with poets, writers, musicians, and others to discuss art and literary movements influencing their creative practices. The movement was to identify and bring out what was within rather than following a particular style or school of art.

The decades of the 1950s and '60s are also seen as a time of identity crises in Indian art based on issues of indigenism versus internationalism.[6] The influence of the Bengal School on existing art practices together with the rejection of semi-classical art taught in colonial art schools was a major shift at this time. Ahmedabad, as a place with strong traditions of handcrafts, was a challenge to this group of young talent who had a shifting sense

1
Portrait of Chhaganlal Jadav. Photograph courtesy Anuj Ambalal.

2
"Untitled", by Chhaganlal Jadav, 1987. Watercolour on paper. Collection: Amit Ambalal.

of aesthetics that would integrate with the aspirations of modernism. This created a gap between the traditionalists and the progressives who explored form and introduced the use of materials other than paint in their work. Artist Jeram Patel used a blowtorch on wooden logs to create abstract masses and painted images on wood, as if the excavated pure forms removed layers of dusty knowledge of art. Through his mastery over the medium, a new meaning was seen in the series of works, marked as progressive by the Indian art scene.

Another student of Ravishankar Raval was Dashrath Patel, the "Dada of Design" who studied painting under Deviprasad Roy Chowdhury at the Government College of Fine Arts, Madras from 1949 to 1953. In the early 1960s Patel joined the National Institute of Design as a faculty member and became a prominent figure in the design world for his photographs, ceramics, and exhibition design. Yet the artistic community saw him as an experimental abstract painter who searched "for form in lines" through various media. According to critic Suneet Chopra, Dashrath Patel transcended painting much beyond the canvas, entering "the much more public world of the open exhibition, the fair, the theatre".[7]

Artists' Studios
One of Chhaganlal's younger contemporaries was Piraji Sagara. Piraji came from a humble Rajasthani background. The family business of refurbishing old furniture provided him with used metal strips, nails, carved panels, and tin sheets with which he began to create his most significant series of collages on wood (figure 3). Inspired by Jeram Patel, he used the blowtorch and paints to make collage paintings, leading artist J. Swaminathan to comment, "Piraji's art is figurative, also textural that builds up the rhythm and movement of imagery. They are not merely visual stimulants; they are also palpable patches of evidence of a culture under travail. They communicate compassion and passion."[8] Piraji, like Jeram Patel before him, was a teacher at the Centre for Environment Planning and Technology (now CEPT University). Preferring to walk to work through the lanes of Ahmedabad every day, he came across men, women, cows, camels, and birds en route. He came to have a predilection for these images as he tried to voice the mystery of life and death, of man and his destiny.[9]

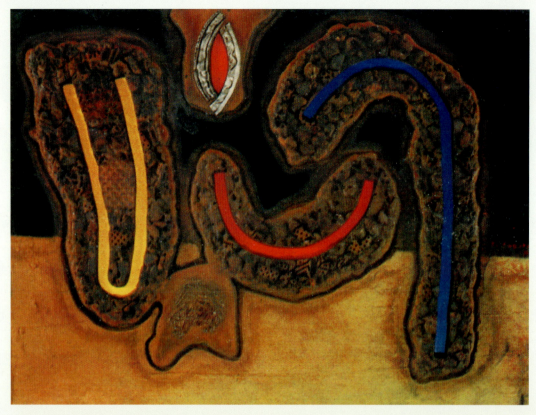

3
"Primitive Signs", by Piraji Sagara, 1964. Burnt wood, metal strips, paint on board, 92 x 122 cm. Photograph courtesy Piraji Sagara Art Foundation.

4
"Music – 2", by Balkrishna Patel, 1996. Oil on canvas, 83.8 x 116.8 cm. Collection: Anil Relia. Photograph courtesy Archer Art Gallery.

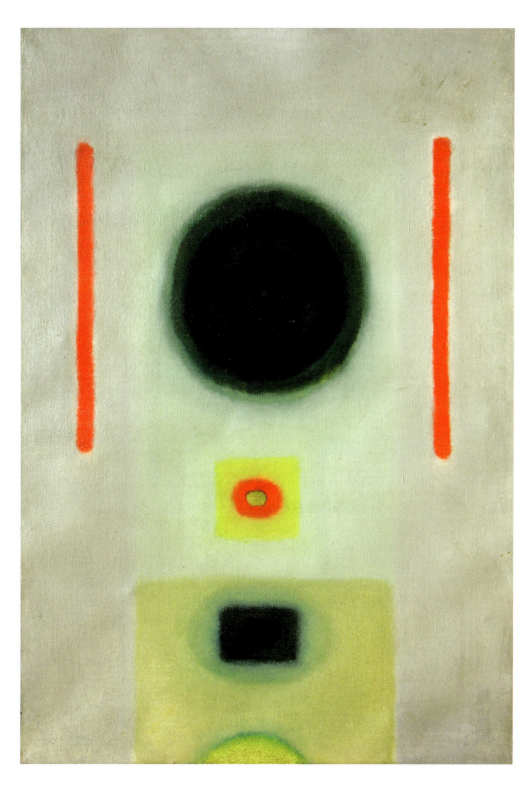

5
"Untitled", by Balkrishna Patel, 1969. Oil on canvas, 106.7 x 73.7 cm. Collection: Anil Relia. Photograph courtesy Archer Art Gallery.

Piraji Sagara's home in the Jamalpur area of the walled city of Ahmedabad was an open studio that was visited by many artists of that time. The young Bhupen Khakhar came quite often and introduced other young artists from Baroda like Gulammohammed Sheikh, Himmat Shah, and Manu Parekh to the Ahmedabad art scene. The studio became "the space" for exchange of ideas between creative minds. Though the C.N. College of Fine Arts was well established under the leadership and guidance of Rasiklal Parikh, there remained a gap between groups that met at the studio and others who studied at the art school.

Another contemporary of Piraji Sagara was Balkrishna Patel who explored pure colours while developing his language through significant abstract paintings. Squares, circles,

and lines in his compositions revealed a meditative quality which represented forms in the most modest manner. Patel's deceptively straightforward, highly evocative works carried subliminal depth (figures 4 and 5). At the same time, Bhanu Shah explored the handcraft of kitemaking, for which Ahmedabad is famous. His kites were his canvas, which also brought the social aspect into his art. The sensibility of this progressive artist was recognized and led to the establishment of a Kite Museum in Ahmedabad. Piraji's younger brother Ishwar Sagara was another promising artist of this time and won the 1973 Triennale Award. Ishwar wove cityscapes and figures to create a world where cognizable forms were rooted in culture to create a visual narrative representing time. This gifted artist tragically died young, not really fulfilling his tremendous potential (figures 6 and 7).

6
"Untitled", by Ishwar Sagara, 1999. Pen and ink on paper, 55.9 x 76.2 cm. Photograph courtesy Piraji Sagara Art Foundation.

7
"Untitled", by Ishwar Sagara, 1998. Pen and ink on paper, 76.2 x 55.9 cm. Photograph courtesy Piraji Sagara Art Foundation.

Art in Private Spaces: City Leaders as Patrons
Ahmedabad is known for having grown under the leadership of its visionary citizens and this is reflected in the city's art scene too. Leading citizens established premier institutes in the early 1960s, such as the National Institute of Design (NID), Indian Institute of Management (IIM), and Centre for Environment Planning and Technology (CEPT). They also invited international artists and designers who interacted with the city and its great heritage in many ways, including designer Charles Eames and architect Louis Kahn from America who worked on various projects in the city which was seen as a cauldron of ideas. Of course, Le Corbusier had already put the city on the world map with his works for private clients as well as for the Ahmedabad Textile Millowners' Association. This later resulted in art residencies at the Sarabhai Foundation, where many European and American masters came and worked.

The Sagara studio, which shifted from Jamalpur to a location on the outskirts of the city, attracted international artists while the Sarabhai Foundation, established by a leading Ahmedabad textile manufacturer, had many European and American masters as resident artists. The list of visitors includes James Rosenquist, Keith Sonnier, Frank Stella, Howard Hodgkin, Isamu Noguchi, Alexander Calder, and Joan Miro; and more recently, Lynda

8
"Untitled", by Anish Kapoor, 1995. Steel and bricks, 0.9 x 0.9 x 0.9 m. Collection: Sarabhai House. Photograph: Rajesh Sagara.

Benglis, David Hockney, Anish Kapoor (figure 8), Long-Bin Chen, and several others. Though many of them came because of their personal contacts with the Sarabhais, others were attracted first to Baroda (Vadodara), the centre of contemporary art in India, and then travelled 100 kilometres north to Ahmedabad.[10] An invitation from the Sarabhai Foundation as well as other patrons from Ahmedabad's elite families was seen by these artists as an opportunity to work in a city with a living history that existed in everyday life – encompassing traditional handcrafts, textiles, architecture, and even Gandhian philosophy. The prospect of staying in the Sarabhai's Le Corbusier-designed house was an added attraction, as well as the easy availability of a variety of materials which is visible in Rauschenberg's as well as Frank Stella's works.[11]

The Sarabhai Foundation invited Robert Rauschenberg to work with paper produced by their mills in 1974. In his essay "Approaching India", art critic and historian Deepak Ananth describes the impact Ahmedabad had on Rauschenberg's work: "Rauschenberg's fascination for colours and fabrics he encountered in Ahmedabad (as attested by his son who accompanied him to India) is registered in the works he made soon after his return to the United States, particularly the 'jammer' series of 1975 that deploy large monochromatic rectangles of silk or satin attached to [a] pole or pinned to the wall, their folds evocative of the rippling of sails or flags – associations that are surely appropriate for the inventor of a pictorial surface that let the world in again."[12]

Contemporary Art Gallery
The city had its first art gallery in 1973 – the Contemporary Art Gallery set up by artist Amit Ambalal. Belonging to a family of textile entrepreneurs, he was always inclined to paint as he watched his mother working under the tutelage of Chhaganlal Jadav. He too began taking lessons from Jadav, who later became his mentor. The Contemporary Art Gallery became the place for local and visiting artists to showcase their works (figures 9 and 11). This space provided an opportunity for students of art schools to experience and understand the contemporary Indian art scene of the time and listen to debates on art and society. Discussing these issues were Gerard Thalmann, a young French artist,

9
Artists Jeram Patel, Bhupen Khakhar, Amit Ambalal, Mansaram, Jyoti Bhatt, Janak Patel, Balkrishna Patel, and Mansing Chhara at Comtemporary Art Gallery, 1974/75. Photograph courtesy Amit Ambalal.

10
"Untitled", collaborative painting by artists of Ahmedabad and visiting artists, 1975. Mixed media on canvas, backyard of Contemporary Art Gallery. Photograph courtesy Amit Ambalal.

11
Artists Amit Ambalal, C.D. Mistry, Piraji Sagara, and Balkrishna Patel at Contemporary Art Gallery, 1983. Photograph courtesy Amit Ambalal.

12
"Untitled", by Amit Ambalal, 2007. Gouache on paper. Photograph courtesy Amit Ambalal.

13
"Khakarnastrix & Co", by Amit Ambalal, 2008. Oil on canvas. Collection: Bodhi Gallery, Delhi. Photograph courtesy Anuj Ambalal.

Modern Art | 89

and the British artist Wowo, both regular visitors who got together with city artists like Ashwin Modi, Bhanu Shah, Mansing Chhara, Janak Patel, and others to create a dialogue between the old and the modern, rural and urban, in a collective installation created in the backyard of the Contemporary Art Gallery (figure 10). This was a 25-foot-long (c. 8-metre) canvas, separated into two parts by painting a totem in the middle, with traditional art on one side and modern art on the other.

Amit Ambalal, a celebrated painter today, has created a place in India's contemporary art scene for his satirical, narrative depictions through the lens of an artist and a commentator. His constant questioning of his own surroundings makes his works most stimulating and thought-provoking (figures 12 and 13). Today his private studio has become a "space" where art is born out of conversations and experiences.

Establishment of Art Centres

The Visual Art Centre (earlier Hutheesing Art Centre) was originally created as a space for the arts and theatre practice where regular experimental theatre performances, poetry readings, and exhibitions were held. The Centre provided a critical ground for melting boundaries and sharing ideas in the fields of music, theatre, and art. Even today it continues to support art activities in the capacity of an art gallery. As the Contemporary Art Gallery and the Visual Art Centre became spaces for artistic pursuits, a larger space for arts and aesthetics was envisaged by the well-known city architect Balkrishna Doshi and artist Piraji Sagara. With generous support from Urmila Kanoria, the Kanoria Centre for Arts was established in 1984 and was also part of CEPT's original idea of bringing art, architecture, and science into close proximity. The Kanoria Centre was a welcome addition to the city's cultural growth that later on became a platform for young, talented artists of the country through its residency programme.

14
"Untitled", by M.F. Husain, 1976. Drawing on paper. Photograph courtesy Amdavad ni Gufa.

15
"Untitled", by M.F. Husain, 1976. Drawing on paper. Photograph courtesy Amdavad ni Gufa.

The Kanoria Centre invited Bhupen Khakhar to interact with art students and conduct an inaugural art and aesthetics workshop in 1984. This was a significant event on the Indian contemporary art scene where art space and residencies were either offered by elite patrons or by the government-sponsored Lalit Kala Akademi in Garhi Studio. The first batch of students in the residency programme included Anita Dube, Krishnakumar, N.N. Rimzon, Yunus Khimani, and Prithpal Singh Ladi. Later Ravinder Reddy joined, on his return from England, and took the Centre's activities to new heights in the early years.

The Kanoria Centre for Arts also became a ground for dialogue among disciplines such as architecture, design, art, and craft, which were linked to contemporary art in India. It provided freedom from academic boundaries, the much needed critical "space" that led many young artists to experiment with materials and mediums.[13] Today the Centre still stands true to its original vision, but the shifts in the art scene, which place a greater emphasis on the patronage to artists by galleries, present a challenge to which the Centre will have to respond. Similarly located in the CEPT campus is a structure which was the result of a conversation between the artist M.F. Husain and the architect Balkrishna Doshi, in 1994. Originally named Husain-Doshi Gufa, it is now known as Amdavad ni Gufa. The free structure was intended as a *gufa* (cave) which could be used as a painter's studio; it now remains as an architectural monument. Adjoining the Gufa is the Herwitz Gallery which provides space for art exhibitions and curated art shows, signifying the shift in patronage from the old, elite families to the domain of the newly rich. The Herwitz Gallery opened with a major show of Husain in 1995 followed by many other prominent names from his generation and other great Indian masters. During the building of Amdavad ni Gufa, Husain was working on his much acclaimed "Theorama" series. At this time he met Anil Relia, a skilled screenprinter who eventually went on to establish the Archer Art Gallery. Today Archer is known for its serigraphic limited-edition reproductions of Indian masters, making art accessible to the common man.

Ahmedabad as a city of individuals has also been decisive about "modernity" as this term stands here within a boundary. It is open to ideas but it could be critical. It accepted Husain's sketches on Ahmedabad city done during the early communal differences. These sketches bring out characteristic images of the city in singular line drawings (figures 14 and 15). The figures here belong to the city environment. These works celebrated the spirit of the city and gained Husain respect for his views, but the same city rejected his works during a show much later that exhibited paintings of Goddess Sarasvati.

A recently opened gallery, Lemongrasshopper (2006), established by a young artist from Baroda, concentrates on new voices from the city and outside, providing a link between the two. Today the gallery has become a window for ceramic arts in the country. Also, Lemongrasshopper chooses to address the issue of art in public spaces in the city by curating shows in such spaces. The recently curated show "Minding the Gap" – installations of sculptures by artist Rajesh Sagara – was set on a heritage route, huge stainless steel and wood sculptures being exhibited at selected spots. This was a significant move to bridge the divide by bringing art to the public (figure 16).

Sarabhai House continues in present times to host artists such as Lynda Benglis, a much celebrated American sculptor who often works from Ahmedabad as the city still remains a place of experimentation, a laboratory that offers the freedom of style or language.[14] The city also invites artists who either belong to it or are visitors passing by intrigued with the city's memories, culture, and spirit. If Rauschenberg took papers and fabrics from here, Ahmedabad continues to stimulate Lynda Benglis to capture patterns of *jalebi* in her works or Long-Bin Chen to make a portrait of Gandhi as one of his reading sculptures.[15] The most recent example of this is Sudarshan Shetty's wood-carved "Cage" (figure 17).[16] The piece is very much inspired by the city's architectural art, the *jali* of the Sidi Saiyyad mosque. This grand piece of fine craftsmanship in architecture is significant in its representation of the history of the city. While the artist has captured this exquisite carving for his show in a museum, it also demonstrates his intention to question historic

16
Installation by Rajesh Sagara from the series "Minding the Gap", 2010. Stainless-steel wire and rexine. Photograph courtesy Lemongrasshopper Art Gallery.

17
"Cage", by Sudarshan Shetty, 2010. Wood, stainless steel. From the exhibition *This Too Shall Pass* at Bhau Daji Lad Museum, Mumbai.

processes, legacies, and primal issues of heritage.[17] Ahmedabad as a cauldron of cultures continues to embrace ideas and cause them to be manifested into great art works.

Notes
1. Ratan Parimoo, *Historical Development of Contemporary Indian Art 1880–1947*, New Delhi: Lalit Kala Akademi, 2009, p. 295.
2. Ravishankar Raval, *Gujarat ma kala na pagrav,* Ahmedabad: Kala Ravi Trust and Archer Art Gallery, 2009, p. 284.
3. Raval 2009, p. 324.
4. Dr Panubhai Bhatt, *Chhaganlal Jadav*: *Catalogue*, Ahmedabad: Gujarat State Lalit Kala Akademi, 1968.
5. Bhatt 1968.
6. Gayatri Sinha, *Amit Ambalal*, Mumbai: Gallery Espace, 2008, p. 54.
7. Suneet Chopra, "Understanding Dashrath Patel", *The Hindu*, Vol. 16, No. 15, 1999. http://www.hindu.com/fline/fl1615/16150820.htm accessed on May 16, 2011.
8. J. Swaminathan, *Piraji Sagara – A Retrospective*, New Delhi: Lalit Kala Akademi, 1982.
9. Swaminathan 1982.
10. Conversation with Anand Sarabhai, Ahmedabad, August 10, 2010.
11. Deepak Ananth, "Approaching India", in *Chalo! India : A New Era of Indian Art*, Karlheinz Essl, Austria: Essl Museum, 2009.
12. Ananth 2009.
13. The Indian art scene needed such laboratory space to accommodate the shifts that took place during the 1990s.
14. In conversation with Lynda Benglis and Anand Sarabhai at Sarabhai House, Ahmedabad, March 22, 2011.
15. Long-Bin Chen, a Taiwanese artist was a resident artist at the Sarabhai Foundation in 2005. He carves works known as "reading sculptures" out of telephone directories and old worn-out books.
16. Sudarshan Shetty, *This Too Shall Pass*, exhibition at Bhau Daji Lad Museum, Mumbai, September 2010.
17. Tasneem Mehta, Curatorial Note, *This Too Shall Pass*.

Food is Serious Business

Sheela Bhatt

Ahmedabad may be 600 years old but Ahmedabadis are young in their food habits. They are madly in love with food. Their moods find expression in food. They vent their emotions through food. The city's social moorings, value system, and rapidly changing lifestyle can be discerned through a survey of the food scene. Arguably, this is so anywhere, but Ahmedabad is a special case. On one plane, the passion for food appears integral to the Ahmedabadi zest for life; on another, it translates into a desperate desire to arrest the ephemeral nature of life. Viewed in another way, by day the Ahmedabadi appears to be a thrifty trader, by night an extravagant epicurean. A third dimension is the austere Ahmedabadi Jain, abstaining from meat and root vegetables, avoiding salt and spices on certain days and fasting on others, or observing food restrictions through the four months of the monsoon season.

Why are Ahmedabadis so food-conscious? Three Ahmedabadis give equally plausible answers to this question. "It must be something to do with this *bhumi* (land)," says Surendra Patel, founder of Vishala, an Ahmedabad-based restaurant serving traditional Gujarati food in the exquisite ambience of a green village. Maybe he is right, for food is the primary language of communication in the city. For instance, when two traders strike a deal in the bustling bazaars they order two "cuttings" (half cups) of masala tea to seal the deal. Labhshankar Thaker, poet and Ayurveda physician (*vaid*), offers another explanation. "Our *shastra*s say that food is the supreme reason for our existence. Perhaps Ahmedabadis have truly internalized this. I am not surprised by Ahmedabadis' zest for good food." Tarak Mehta, popular satirist, adds, "Gujaratis have a fetish for eating out. Like religion and money, food is the centre-point of our life."

Eating Out

Yet, it appears that the zest for eating out is a new phenomenon. Writer Vinod Bhatt recalls the days, just a few decades ago, when parents were orthodox and frugal. They would not even drink water in a restaurant. Youngsters were told to eat without fuss the food cooked at home – the typical Gujarati meal of *dal-bhat-rotli-shak-ane-mithai* or lentils, rice, bread, vegetable, and sweet.

Many of the items in the traditional Gujarati meal have been eaten since medieval times (figure 1). The 15th-century text *Varnakasamuchchaya*, written around the time Ahmedabad was established, describes food items made from wheat, rice, bajra and gram; *idli* or *idri* now regarded as a South Indian snack was known from the 12th century onwards. Similarly *khandvi*, *wadi*, and *papad* were made at home and this tradition has continued. The late-16th-century Gujarati text *Jimanvar Paridhan Vidhi* lists 36 kinds of *laddu*s and sweets such as *khaja*, *lapsi*, *sukhdi*, and *dhoodhpak* which are still popular today as is the *jalebi* introduced in the 15th century.[1]

1
Street vendors selling a special selection of cut vegetables offered to Lord Krishna on Janmashtami. Photograph: Jinal Patel.

The shift to eating out was conservative in the beginning. What was sought in a restaurant was food that tasted just like the homemade items. Traditional Ahmedabadis, famous for their extreme shrewdness, started paying for *ghar jevun khavanu* (food that tastes like it is home-cooked). Like the excellent Gujarati *dal* at Chandravilas with its perfect sweet-sour proportion. Or *dal-dhokli* at Khadia's Purohit Hotel. Vinod Bhatt says the customer in "those days" was king. They would order "cuttings", ask for a free copy of the day's newspaper, instruct the waiter to make the fan go faster, and also to keep an eye on their cycles!

The first non-Gujarati food to find favour with young people was Azad Halwai's *puri-shak* and *dal-pakwan* made by a Sindhi refugee. *Chhole-puri* at Havmor and Sankalp Hotel's *dosa*s were also popular. Havmor was established by Satish Chona in Karachi in 1944. After Partition he settled in Ahmedabad, restarting his business by selling hand-churned ice-cream at the railway station. Later he expanded to a chain of Havmor restaurants serving ice-cream and Punjabi food with *acchai-sachhai-safai*, goodness-honesty-cleanliness, as the cornerstone of the business (figure 2).[2] Havmor also came to be a refuge for young couples seeking privacy from the joint family dinner table.

There was another kind of "eating out" which had roots older than the middle-class patronage of restaurants. With the establishment of mills in the late 19th century, food stalls sprung up to cater to the needs of workers. Night stalls came up to serve inexpensive food to workers on their way home or on their way to the mills for the night shift. The night-time eateries of Manek Chowk, which transform the business district of the walled city into a carnival of food at night, originated to serve this need (figures 3a and b). Some stalls became famous – Raipur Bhajiya House at Raipur Darwaza, *bhajiyas* at Vadigam, *samosa* and *khasta kachori* sold by vendors at Madhupura Darwaza, the *chavana* at the old Stock Exchange – and, over time, became landmarks in the food geography of the city. Eating at these stalls continued long after the mills closed down in the 1980s. In the city spread over the two banks of the river Sabarmati, there are thousands of food stalls on the wayside and pavements (figures 4a and b) with each locality having its own "famous" ones – *pav-bhaji* at Vasna, near Paldi-Bhaththa; the Karnavati area's *dabeli*; *panipuri* outside Parekh's departmental store at Lal Darwaza.

Sheela Bhatt

2
Advertisement hoarding for Havmor ice-cream. Photograph: Hanif Sindhi.

3a
A night view of Manek Chowk transformed into an eatery, with a backdrop of jewellery shops. Photograph: Hanif Sindhi.

3b
Selling fried savouries and *chat*, Manek Chowk. Photograph: Hanif Sindhi.

4a
Safe Food, Tasty Food: vendors selling fusion food. Photograph: Hanif Sindhi.

4b
Chat and *panipuri* vendor. Photograph: Hanif Sindhi.

Vegetarianism and Eating Meat

The followers of Jainism, besides being vegetarian, observe a range of strict food restrictions. Their religion prohibits the eating of all underground vegetables including potatoes, onions, garlic, ginger, carrots, radish, and the like, as well as fermented foods. During several religious festivals all green vegetables are also prohibited and on some of these, even oil and spices. Within the restrictions imposed by their religion, Jains have developed a cuisine in which the same Gujarati food preparations have a more delicate taste because of the absence of strong-smelling onions, garlic, and ginger. Responding to the restrictions on green vegetables at certain times of the year, Jain food has a range of dried lentil preparations like *papad*, *wadi*, and *ganthia* which replace vegetables. Even with restrictions on vegetables and spices during the *ayambil* fast, Jains have innovated a range of "fasting versions" of *idli-dosa*, *sambar*, *panipuri*, *bhelpuri*, and *kachori*, skilfully making a feast out of the fast.

Gujarat's wealthy Jain minority has been very influential for centuries, and their clout in the economic and political arena has had an impact in the arena of food as well, particularly in the matter of eating meat. For instance, under their influence, the 12th-century Solanki king Kumarapal forbade the killing of animals in Gujarat. Even during Mughal times Jains were able to get the emperors to forbid the killing of animals during their holy month of Paryushan and the community has continued to campaign quite successfully for this ban with elected representatives to this day. Multinational food chains too have had to bow to the city's powerful vegetarian ethic, with Pizza Hut starting operations here by opening its first all-vegetarian outlet in the world. Nestle has recently introduced a Jain version of their popular Maggi instant noodles!

The Swaminarayan sect of Hindus observes an equally strict vegetarian diet though it is restricted to avoiding onions and garlic, while the Vaishnavas observe no restrictions within their basic vegetarianism. The cultural impact of the Jain, Vaishnava, and Swaminarayan food ethic is so powerful that even today migrant families from meat-eating communities find it impossible to rent houses in their localities. Most grocery shops in the vicinity of these localities do not sell eggs; the few that do keep them out of sight and a customer wishing to buy eggs has to euphemistically ask for "white potatoes". And most restaurants feature Jain versions of the items on their menu – which means that not only are these vegetarian but also prepared without garlic, onions, and other prohibited vegetables.

5a
Preparation of *manda roti* in Bhatiyar Gali. Photograph: Hanif Sindhi.

5b
Preparing *tandoori roti*s in Bhatiyar Gali. Photograph: Jinal Patel.

So do Ahmedabadis eat meat? Yes, they do, despite the seemingly overwhelming vegetarian ethic. In the central business area of the old walled core of the city is Bhatiyar Gali which is the main meat market. Mutton, chicken, fish, and eggs are sold here and the market is patronized by rich and poor. Cooked foods are also sold here, starting with the early morning *paya* soup – a clear soup made from trotters, a delicacy which is also believed to relieve bone ailments and so sought-after by many who suffer from arthritis and other orthopaedic problems. Through the day gravies are prepared and meat is readied, and by night, the area transforms into a lively eating area serving mainly Mughlai preparations

5c
Barahandi in Bhatiyar Gali.
Photograph: Jinal Patel.

made on the *tawa* and *tandoor* (figures 5a–c). The most famous is the *barahandi*, or 12 vessels, each with a preparation of a different kind of meat – trotters, kidney, liver, chicken, mutton, and so on.

Other areas of the city have their own specialties, indicating how widespread the eating of meat really is in Ahmedabad. The mutton *biryani* at Jamalpur, and meat fries at Astodia Darwaza, Lucky's mutton *samosa*s at Mirzapur and near the Pir Muhammad Shah dargah off Relief Road are all famous in the old walled core of the city. In the industrial area of Ahmedabad, where the mills once hummed, fried meat preparations at Usha Theatre in

Gomtipur are still relished. Two Goan restaurants, in Mirzapur and Lal Darwaza, added to the variety: Greens, which no longer exists, was famous for fried fish while La Bella continues to serve inexpensive beef and mutton dishes.

Ahmedabad's Bohra and Memon Muslim communities and the Parsis have their special cuisines where meat preparations use different spices. Memon cooking tends to be spicier and incorporates many vegetarian Gujarati chutneys, pickles, and *papad*. Bohra cuisine is lightly spiced and the local *bajra* cereal is incorporated into some preparations. A practice unique to Bohra feasts is that the meal starts with ice-cream and sweets. The Parsis too have their unique *dhansak* which is a mixture of lentils, vegetables, and meat. An unusual feature of Bohra and Memon meals is that families eat together from one large platter, a practice unknown in other communities. Yet, none of these specialties has found its way into restaurant menus or street food, and they remain restricted to family kitchens, except perhaps for a vegetarian version of *dhansak* which has recently appeared on the menus of a few Ahmedabad restaurants.

Variety is the Spice
Ahmedabad has absorbed non-local food for several centuries. The Portuguese brought their *pao* or bread, the Mughals brought their cuisine, tea was introduced in the early 20th century, and Sindhi and Punjabi refugees acquainted Ahmedabadis with their food. In fact today, the Sindhis dominate the restaurant business in Ahmedabad in a big way. In the last 10 or 12 years, the kind of fusion taking place in the kitchens of city restaurants is mind-boggling. A hotchpotch, multi-cuisine food scene has emerged with mutant varieties of national and international food entering restaurants and finding a place in wedding celebrations.

Even street stalls offer a wide range of specialties from the rest of the country – Mumbai, South India, Punjab, Northeast India – and international cuisine from Lebanon, Tibet, Mexico, China, Thailand, Italy, albeit localized in taste and spice. So Jasuben's pizza has a base resembling the thick, crisp Gujarati *bhakhri* made of wheat, with sweetened tomato puree and a mountain of unbaked local Amul cheese as topping. In fact, Jasuben's Pizza has a page on Facebook with a huge following. Many of these items have made their way to the city's palate through diaspora Ahmedabadis living in the United States and exposed to food from all over the world. It is not unusual to now find, in neighbourhood grocery stores,

6
Distribution of sprouted mung as *prasad* during the Jagannath *rath-yatra*. Photograph: Hanif Sindhi.

7
Breaking Ramzan fast at the Jama Masjid. Photograph: Hanif Sindhi.

different varieties of pasta, pitted olives, bottles of Schezwan and pizza sauces, while roadside vegetable vendors stock broccoli, basil leaves, lettuce, and sometimes even asparagus.

An NGO organizes a food festival on the campus of the Indian Institute of Management every winter, where farmers from the tribal areas of Gujarat come and make their staple foods. In just two days each farmer is able to take home about a lakh of rupees from selling *nagli* flour, sweet bamboo *halwa*, and *bawta ladu*s. In fact, more and more, the rich seem to want to eat the poor man's food – as a result of which minor millets are sold in many upmarket grocery stores.

But the craze for non-local varieties has seriously affected the quality of traditional Gujarati items. It is very difficult to get authentic *churmana ladu* (sweet made of flour, ghee, and sugar) or even *dhokla*s. Even an authentic *thali* is hard to find now as Punjabi, Chinese, and Mexican food infiltrate what was the stronghold of traditional Gujarati fare. In fact upmarket *thali* restaurants serve mildly spiced versions including Western variations of local vegetables cooked in bechamel sauce to cater to foreign tourists.

Yet many traditions continue, such as the food served as blessing at the temples and dargahs of Ahmedabad. Twice a year, *annakut* (mountain of food) and *chappanbhog* (56 kinds of food) are offered to Lord Krishna and later distributed to devotees as *prasad* (blessing) (see figure 1). During the *rath-yatra* of Lord Jagannath, boiled mung beans, *ganthia* (fried snack made of chickpea flour), and *malpua* (sweet made of wheat flour, sugar, and ghee) are distributed along the route of the god's tour through the city (figure 6). Similarly, at the *urs* celebrations of the major saints of Ahmedabad, food is distributed at their dargahs in the city. At Sheikh Ahmed Khattu's *urs*, *khichda* made of wheat and lentils is distributed in Sarkhej, at Shah Alam's *urs* there are *ladu*s, and the dargah of Pir Muhammad Shah is famous for its *pulao* (a preparation made of rice known as Pir Muhammad Shah *pulao*) at the time of the saint's *urs*. During Ramzan, *halim* of wheat, lentils, and meat is served to devotees who come to recite an extra night-time prayer at this dargah. Devotees also gather at mosques to pray and to break their fast (figure 7).

The Business of Food

The Ahmedabadi's craving for varieties of food has made the food business a popular one. Balkrishna Nair has a stall in Manek Chowk in the heart of the traditional business area. He came to the city a decade ago from Kerala with his football team. And he stayed on. From selling *idli-dosa* on a bench in the old city, today he has his own house and is all set to finance his son's business. The yearly food bill of Ahmedabadi families passionate about "eating out" is more than Rs 1,500 crore, says Narendra Somani, Sindhi owner of The Grand Bhagwati, who started selling Delhi *chat* and other North Indian fare on the roadside and is now the owner of a very successful chain of vegetarian restaurants. It is very common to read rags-to-riches stories about street food vendors earning lakhs and owning bungalows in posh areas.

But nowhere is food innovation and entrepreneurship more apparent than in wedding feasts. In a state where consumption of liquor is prohibited by law, food becomes the arena where the growing class of affluent Ahmedabadis exhibit their wealth, spending thousands of rupees on the food served at their wedding celebrations. Wedding caterers reveal that a meal for a single guest at an elite wedding could consist of ten starters, fifteen kinds of salads and chutneys, ten types of drinks and sherbets, and an entire range of Punjabi and Gujarati food in the main course with separate corners for Thai, Italian, and Chinese food and for the street food of New Delhi, finished off with about ten varieties of desserts from different parts of the world. Even middle-class and lower-middle-class marriage receptions have now begun to feature Chinese noodles and pasta.

Entrepreneurship and variety can be observed in street food too, and can go to unimaginable limits. One such offering is the pineapple sandwich which is a combination of bread, butter, cheese, and pineapple rings – the most popular item in Manek Chowk, the city's hot spot for street food (figure 8). In Vastrapur, roadside *panipuri* stalls sell this local snack with eight types of flavoured water to go with the *puri*s, that includes garlic and onion flavour too. It appears that giving an excess of choices is essential for success in the food business. In another famous "food lane", Law Garden, Nathu Pradhan of Ajay Food Stall, serving Punjabi and Chinese food, sums up the situation, "People here are so

8
Pineapple Sandwich at Manek Chowk. Photograph: Hemali Mehta.

9
Vishala Utensils Museum.
Photograph: Dinesh Shukla.

shaukeen (enthusiastic) that even at 1.30 a.m. they force me to keep my stall open." And Ahmedabad even has a museum dedicated to utensils (figure 9).

The Unhealthy Ahmedabadi
The fervour for food has a darker side. Poet and *vaid* Labhshankar Thaker reveals that 40 to 50 per cent of his patients are overweight. According to him, people's food habits are wrong, they are not walking enough to sustain their intake and they eat but are unable to digest their food properly. In such a situation, along with restaurants and food stalls, clinics offering nature cures, Ayurvedic treatment, and weight loss advice have proliferated. Some entrepreneurs have also spotted a business opportunity in home delivery of diet food tailored to dieticians' recommendations, with a clientele among the well-to-do.

Perhaps the only Ahmedabadi who was conscious about healthy eating was Mahatma Gandhi. Sabarmati Ashram became a site for his experiments not only with truth but also with food. He tried naturopathy, Jain food regimens, and fasting. In fact, *aswad* (control of the palate) was one of the vows that each person living in the ashram had to take. Of course, his rules were not popular with his family and colleagues at the ashram and it was Kasturba who mediated and persuaded her husband to be a little more flexible about food! Gandhi is gone and his influence in Ahmedabad has waned in most matters. Vinod Bhatt sums up the food culture of his city through his insight into the philosophy of Ahmedabadis: "The issue is simple. *Khavamanthi anand ave chhe. Khavun ane kamavu, tej jivanchhe* – Food gives pleasure. Eating and earning – that is what life is about!"

Acknowledgements
This essay was written with the generous support of Surendra Patel (interviewed on November 16, 2010), Labhshankar Thaker (interviewed on December 3, 2010), Tarak Mehta (interviewed on January 16, 2011), Vinod Bhatt (interviewed on January 17, 2011), Balkrishna Nair (interviewed on February 2, 2011), Narendra Somani (interviewed on February 3, 2011), Asif Sheikh and Zarine Mirza (interviewed on March 28, 2011), and Rushad Ginwala (interviewed on April 11, 2011).

Notes
1. G. Sandesara Bhogilal (ed.), *Varnakasamuchchaya*, 2 parts, Baroda: M.S. University, 1956–59, pp. 11, 261.
2. http://www.havmor.com/about_us_history.html accessed on March 9, 2011.

The Legend of Sabarmati's Hand-Blockprinted Textiles

Aditi Ranjan

During the short months of the monsoon, a sheet of heavy rain would envelop the city's skyline in tonalities of grey, and the swirling waters of the serpentine Sabarmati would bring to a halt several livelihoods dependent on the sandy riverbed. As the monsoon receded, men and women belonging to the nomadic Ode community of traditional pastoralists would drive a herd of donkeys to fetch sand from the riverbed and transport it to construction sites in the new city on the western bank. The Ode woman's braided hairstyle and her elegant stride in her heavily gathered skirt made of blockprinted stripes and drawstrings decorated with cowrie shells reminded you that the varied folk communities of Gujarat and Rajasthan were patrons of the region's textile expressions. In the months until the next monsoon, the Sabarmati riverbed would come alive as Ahmedabad's textile narrative unfolded on her sands. The flowing waters of the river were useful for washing the excess dye from freshly dyed textiles and blockprinted fabrics. The sun and the dry sandbed with its moist lower layers were ideal for drying and bleaching *kora* or undyed cloth in preparation for blockprinting. The riverbed would become a painter's canvas with patches of white fabric spread out beside yellow, red, and multicoloured and patterned textiles, made timeless through the photographs of Henri Cartier-Bresson and Dashrath Patel from the 1960s (figures 1–5). Blockprinted fabrics drying on the riverbed were iconic of the Sabarmati in Ahmedabad up until the 1980s when the Vasna barrage and Narmada canal enabled the river to retain water through the year, altering these visual narratives.

The Sabarmati has witnessed hundreds of years of the painted and printed textile traditions since at least the medieval period when textiles were exported from the port of Cambay or Khambhat to Greece, Egypt, Indonesia, Siam or modern-day Thailand, and Yemen. The textile and maritime trade traditions of Gujarat share a common ancient ancestry characterized by globalization. Several historians and scholars have written about the silk Patola, embroidered and resist-dyed fabrics, and blockprinted textiles that were made in Gujarat for export to Egypt, Southeast Asia, and Europe. Not only were the skills for creating and producing textiles extant in Gujarat but there was also a network of inland routes leading to the ports at Surat, Khambhat, and Bharuch and thus to overseas trade routes.

Blockmaking at Pethapur, blockprinting of Saudagiri textiles for export to Thailand, and the blockprinting and painting traditions of Mata ni Pachedi are closely linked to the Sabarmati river. The position of Ahmedabad in the pre-industrial age as an important

1
The Sabarmati was a rainfed river with islands of sand. In the 1960–70s blockprinters would bring their fabrics to the riverbed and dyers would dye the fabrics red, using wooden barrels. The fabrics were then washed in running water and dried on the sand. Photograph: Dashrath Patel, courtesy National Institute of Design (NID).

2
Cotton fabrics printed in the *patri* or chemical black discharge technique being dried on the riverbed during the 1960s. Photograph: Dashrath Patel, courtesy NID.

3
A bird's-eye view of the Sabarmati riverbed in the 1960s. The patchwork of textiles drying on the sand evokes the memory of dyers' and washermen's activities. The river was the lifeline of the hand-blockprinting industry in Ahmedabad. Photograph: Dashrath Patel, courtesy Dashrath Patel Museum.

4
Many textile narratives unfolded on the Sabarmati riverbed. Here, the washerman and his family members have laid out blockprinted cotton fabrics to dry, while undyed fabric has been desized, washed, and set aside for drying. Photograph: Dashrath Patel, courtesy NID.

5
Cotton fabrics dyed red and washed, laid out to dry on the riverbed in the 1960s. Photograph: Dashrath Patel, courtesy NID.

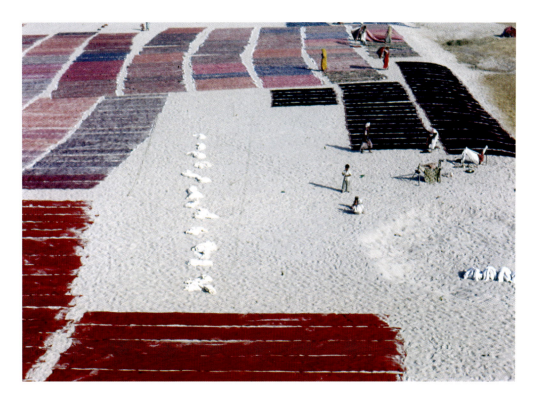

textile and trade centre was due to the synergetic interaction between traders, dyers, weavers, blockprinters, washermen, calenderers, and the folk communities of Gujarat who used these textiles. In the 17th century, Sarkhej was well known for cultivating and exporting indigo.[1] Ahmedabad was founded in 1411 and by 1487 it was developed into a walled enclosure with 16 monumental stone gates ornamented with delicate carvings.[2] The pols or gated dwellings where people of the same community could reside attracted craftsmen and traders to settle in Ahmedabad. Some of the craftsmen were silk and cotton weavers, dyers, and *chhipa*s or blockprinters.[3]

6
A four-colour Saudagiri design which has been starched and glazed. The size and scale of the geometric pattern is small. These textiles were produced for Maskati & Co. in the 19th century. From the private collection of Yasin Savaijiwala. Photograph: M.P. Ranjan.

7
A two-colour Saudagiri design printed on cotton fabric by Yasin Savaijiwala's grandfather for Maskati & Co. for export to Thailand in the 19th century. The border is made of rows of floral forms which end in the long spires characteristic of textile designs preferred in Thailand. From the private collection of Yasin Savaijiwala. Photograph: M.P. Ranjan.

Saudagiri Prints and Blockmaking at Pethapur

A group of cotton printed and glazed fabrics called Saudagiri, or "trade goods" were made in Ahmedabad in the 19th century for export to Thailand. This was an example of design for export: local skills harnessed to create patterns that appealed to the sensibilities of markets in a distant land. The Saudagiri designs were small geometrical and floral patterns with a distinctive border, and were printed in two, three, or four colours covering the entire surface of the fabric (figures 6 and 7). The structure of the pattern was a rhombic grid, which was elaborated with stylized leaf and flower forms, sometimes with a flower in the centre of the rhombus or rhombic-shaped motifs placed in the grid.

The *chhipa*s of Ahmedabad (as also in Bagru, Bagh, and other centres of blockprinting) had developed a unique way of recording and sampling all their blocks and colour variations on a single textile. Inspired by the blockprinter's sampler, Martand Singh commissioned a "design directory", an almanac of 100 tradition-based variations in one tiled display, for the *Festival of India* exhibitions which spanned 1982–92 – an exposition and revival of traditional crafts (figure 8).[4]

Damodar Gajjar, mastercraftsman, blockmaker and printer, and an artist from the Fine Arts faculty of M.S. University in Vadodara, recounts a possible origin of Saudagiri prints. An Indian trader in Thailand belonging to Maskati & Co., a trading company of Surat, noticed that finely printed cotton fabrics were being exported from India's Coromandal coast for Thailand's royal family and the ruling elite. He saw the opportunity to develop printed fabrics for the common people in Thailand who wore a draped style of lower and upper garments. During a visit to his hometown Surat he travelled to Ahmedabad where he encouraged innovation of a multicolour printed, starched, and glazed cotton fabric that simulated silk. The full area of the fabric was covered with the hand-blockprint, and its highly starched surface was rubbed with an *aqiq* or agate stone which gave it a lustre. Up until 1980, artisans in the Khadia area of Ahmedabad have been observed giving a finish to printed saris by rubbing the surface with an agate stone.[5] The Maskati trader had probably chosen Ahmedabad as it had blockprinters and tie-dye craftsmen who had moved there because of the Sabarmati river. Ahmedabad was known for producing inexpensive printed fabrics in the 17th century.[6] Perhaps the term Saudagiri was indicative of the *saudagar* or a trader being the driving force behind exporting the skills of blockmakers and printers to Thailand.

8
A part of the design directory created using 100 blocks and synthetic dyes to reinterpret the Saudagiri sensibility for the *Festival of India* exhibition in Britain 1982. It uses a resist block in each square and contains the entire vocabulary of the Pethapur blockmakers in the Saudagiri tradition. Photograph courtesy Vishwakarma Collection.

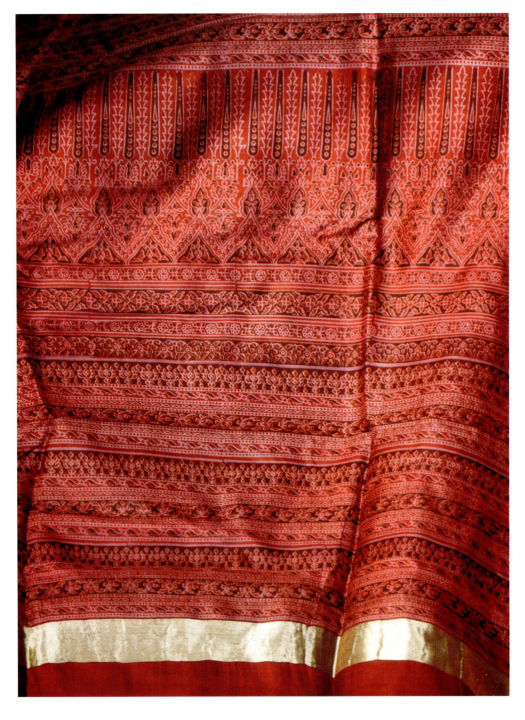

9
A detail of a silk sari designed by Damodar Gajjar who belongs to a family of blockcarvers of Pethapur. He was commissioned to develop a collection of designs to revive Saudagiri designs for the National Design Collection in the 1980s.

10 (opposite)
Seen here is the carved face of an outline block called *rekh* of the border of a Saudagiri design. The block has a large handle which is not visible here that enables the printer to manipulate the block. This intricately carved block belongs to Damodar Gajjar, given to him by one of his family members. He recounted that Sag wood was procured from the Dang forests in south Gujarat, processed by sawmills in Dharampur, seasoned and prepared for making the block. The wood was purchased by the society of blockcarvers in Pethapur. Photograph: Aditi Ranjan.

    Pethapur, located on the banks of the Sabarmati about 40 kilometres from Ahmedabad, was well known for its professional blockmakers who carved blocks for printers in Ahmedabad, Deesa, Kutch, Jaipur, and other blockprinting centres in Rajasthan and Madhya Pradesh (figures 9–11). An article in *India Magazine* by Professor Jyotindra Jain[7] brought to light the symbiotic relationship between the trading companies called Maskati, Vasi, and Baghwall in Surat, blockcarvers in Pethapur, and blockprinters in Ahmedabad which had made Pethapur prosperous and sustained the export of Saudagiri prints in large quantities to Thailand from 1850 to 1940.

    The legendary Saudagiri prints, which had given an impetus to the blockcarving craft of Pethapur, are displayed in one section of the Textile Techniques Gallery at the Calico Museum of Textiles in Ahmedabad. The section "Wooden Blocks for Printing" in the Gallery documents the blockprinting traditions of Gujarat exemplified by Mata ni

Pachedi, *ajrak*, and Saudagiri textiles; also displayed are blocks from Bagru and Sanganer in Rajasthan and large, carved wooden blocks with intricate patterns used in clamp resist-dyed textiles. The Museum has dedicated an entire section to the master-craftsman awardee Maneklal Gajjar. The text panels are in Gujarati with technical description of the blockcarving process along with diagrams and actual blocks, several of the blocks having been carved by Maneklal Gajjar.

Maneklal Gajjar and many generations of blockmakers of Pethapur could be considered the custodians of this craft, maintaining records of blocks carved and the names of their clients. Maneklal Gajjar had a pattern book of Saudagiri prints left to him by his ancestors. The annotated pattern book was a meticulous record of the designs with impressions of the blocks carved, names of printers, and traders' logos and labels. The scope of the blockmaker's abilities broadened, from reproduction of old fragments or paper references to visualizing a printer's requirement and creating new surface designs and developing variations. The blockcarver became so perfect in his understanding that he would rectify the printer or customer's motif or surface in consonance with the grammar of print design, the type of fabric, and the technique of printing. Maneklal Gajjar's passion for his craft has given him the immense patience to share with all kinds of people the intricacies of blockmaking. He has shown, with pride, impressions of the Saudagiri blocks to every textile enthusiast, scholar, and tourist visiting Pethapur over the years. Today this ageing National Awardee is a widower with failing eyesight, which has forced him to close his workshop.

Maneklal Gajjar used to proudly recount his father's skills in developing designs that were appreciated by buyers in Thailand. Original samples came from Thailand on a yellow paper with designs drawn in black outline, and his father would be asked by the manager of the trading company to make variations of the designs. The blockmaker's creativity lay in understanding the basic geometric structure and introducing floral elements, thus maintaining its suitability for the technique while offering new viable surface designs. These were sent back to Thailand for feedback and often returned with approval, ensuring orders for the blockcarvers of Pethapur and the blockprinters of Ahmedabad.[8] This smooth coordination between groups in Gujarat and overseas was managed by the trading

11

A set of three blocks of the Saudagiri border design carved according to the number of colours used. Precision tools such as chisels, wooden mallet, bow drill, and punches were used for carving, file and sandpaper for smoothening the surface, and a planer and saw for preparing the wood. The hallmark of Pethapur's blocks was that the pattern to be printed was carved in high relief. This ensured that the block picked up colour only in intricately carved areas and not in unwanted areas. From the collection of Damodar Gajjar in Vadodara. Photograph: Aditi Ranjan.

HAND-BLOCKPRINTED TEXTILES | 113

companies in Surat who were said to have had entrepreneurial-cum-welfare interests in the artisan communities engaged in producing Saudagiri prints.[9]

Saudagiri designs have stopped being produced for export since 1940. However, Ahmedabad's links with the legendary designs are still alive. Yasin Savaijiwala, whose family had produced Saudagiri prints for Maskati & Co. in Surat for three generations, wanted to revive Saudagiri designs. In 2005, using references from Maneklal Gajjar's register, he got 20 wooden blocks carved by blockmakers in Isanpur on the outskirts of Ahmedabad. These blockmakers had migrated from Uttar Pradesh to Ahmedabad. Yasinbhai, aware of the present bleak market reality in Ahmedabad, awaits an opportunity to develop a Saudagiri design collection by collaborating with a designer. Maneklal Gajjar's modest archival record (handed down from father to son) of Saudagiri designs has become an invaluable resource, enabling a printer in 2005 to reproduce the old designs.

Blockprinting Traditions

Ahmedabad is home to many artisans – traditional dyers and printers from Gujarat and Rajasthan, as well as zari and zardozi embroiderers from Allahabad and Kanpur and blockmakers from Farrukhabad in Uttar Pradesh. The enterprising cloth merchants of Ahmedabad also retailed the typical blockprints worn by folk communities of Saurashtra, north Gujarat, and Rajasthan who had migrated to Ahmedabad for work. In the 1970s, cloth merchants near Rani no Hajiro in Manek Chowk, the neighbourhood market in the old walled city, specialized in selling resist-dyed blockprints or *cheent* from Deesa, *ajrak* from Kutch, and blockprints from Bagru and Sanganer in Rajasthan. Also, cloth merchants in Madhavpura sourced *cheent* from Pipad in Rajasthan, making Ahmedabad a hub for blockprinted fabrics. Ahmedabad's printed textiles were also quite differentiated: the *chayal* or blockprinted *odhani* worn by Thakore and Patel communities and tribal communities of Chhota Udaipur; the *chiddri* and *pomcha* sari worn by widows. The *chayal* was done in three-colour variations using *buta*s or large motifs and borders, with a *lehar* or wave pattern printed in the body (figures 12–15). The *chiddri* had a border and small motifs printed in black or blue on a white ground, symbolic of sorrow and mourning. The black and red resist-dyed *nagariya sadlo* or sari was worn by widows of the Thakore, Prajapati, Patel, and Vania communities (figure 16). The technique consisted of dyeing the fabric red, printing the pattern block using mud as a resist, and then dyeing it black or deep indigo. When this dyed fabric was washed to remove the mud, the pattern was revealed in red on a dark

12
A reinterpretation of the traditional *chayal* developed by Ahmedbhai Gamthiwala in the 1980s. He recalls the large motif as *jhadwala buta*. The *buta* block and the stripes used in his reinterpretation are distinctive of the textiles printed in Ahmedabad. The printers created several variations based on permutations and combinations of the stripes and buta blocks, plain fields, and fields printed with different patterns beside the *lehar* used here. Photograph: M.P. Ranjan.

14
The *rekh* or outline block of the *jhadwala buta* from the private collection of Damodar Gajjar. Felt has been filled in the centre of the flower forms for even transfer of colour onto the cloth. Photograph: Aditi Ranjan.

13
The *gaddh* or background block of the *jhadwala buta* or tree motif. Wool fibre or felt has been ingeniously used by the blockmaker and embedded in the entire ground around the *jhadwala buta* to enhance the even absorption of the colour over a large area. In case this was only wood the colour would have been patchy and uneven, whereas the felt has improved the colour-carrying capacity of the block. The *pavan sar* or air vents located in the block prevent the fabric from being lifted with the block. From the private collection of Damodar Gajjar. Photograph: Aditi Ranjan.

15
Impression of the *jhadwala buta* in the pattern book belonging to Damodar Gajjar that was given to him by a member of his extended family of blockmakers in Pethapur in the 19th century. Photograph: Aditi Ranjan.

16
Cotton *nagariya sadlo* or sari worn by widows. From the private collection of Damodar Gajjar. Photograph: Aditi Ranjan.

17
Cotton *odhani* or veil cloth called *madrasia* which simulates the tie-dye technique. From the private collection of Krishna Amin Patel. Photograph: M.P. Ranjan.

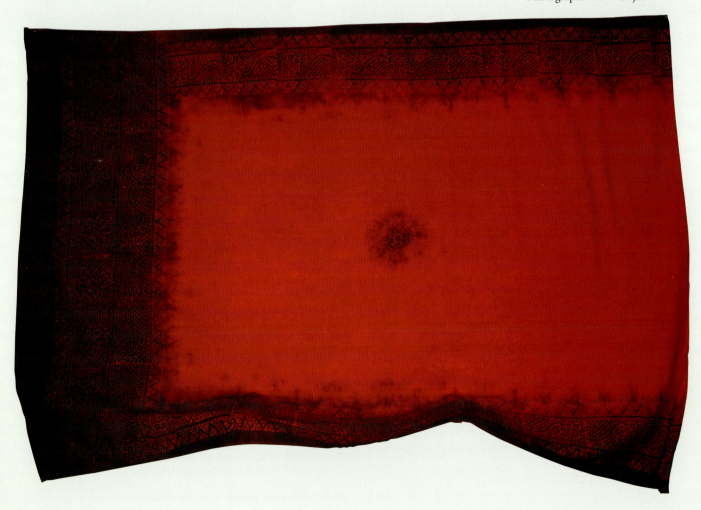

ground. *Odhani*s or veil cloths in red and black called *jimmi* and *madrasia* were worn by Thakarda women (figure 17). The designs simulated the tie-dyed patterns of Kutch and Saurashtra which form an important part of the clothing traditions of these regions.

Traditional *odhani*s and saris were printed by the *chhipa* community living in Chhipawad, the residence of *chhipa*s or blockprinters who had migrated here from Rajasthan 100 years ago.[10] This was the city's largest cluster of skilled artisans, evidence of Ahmedabad being an important textile printing centre. In the 1970s, Chhipawad had an organized assembly-line way of production that was carried out by various groups.[11] The *chhipa*s were women and five or six of them reported to a *chhipa*-turned-manager who supervised all the tasks, from procuring the grey fabric to supplying the printed goods. After the fabrics were cut according to the products to be printed, they were taken to the riverbed for washing and drying. On returning, each *chhipa* would print one block and pass it on to the next *chhipa* for the second step in the printing sequence. The *chhipa*-supervisor would ingeniously plan to print two *odhani*s (each of 2.25 metres) with their *cheda* or borders facing each other, or one sari (of 4.5 metres) on pre-cut fabrics. The fabrics thus printed in naphthol colours were taken back to the riverbed. A dyer would develop the printed fabrics in a naphthol base in a wooden barrel, followed by a final washing in the river. *Odhani*s and saris were printed on an inexpensive *mulmul* or fine cotton fabric. It is interesting to note that even a medium-priced product required several skill sets – that of the supervisor, the *chhipa*, the dyer, and the washerman. Chhipawad's printers are almost nonexistent today and the craft of blockprinting has been severely impacted by the millmade screenprinted polyester fabric which has squeezed out the market for cotton textiles.

Roghan

Roghan printing was the blockprinter's innovation to offer an affordable substitute for gold- and silk-brocaded fabric. A tradition of Rajasthan, *roghan* refers to *chappai ka gum* or a natural adhesive for printing made of a mixture of castor oil residue, titanium dioxide, and turpentine. The tradition of *roghan* printing enabled the printing of gold and silver dust, gold and silver foil, tinsel, and fibre dust or flock on a wide range of fabrics. It was earlier called *abrak chappai* or printing with mica powder which created the tinsel effect. *Roghan* printing was done on flags, standards, velvet tent hangings, cradle cloths, and book covers (figure 18).

Hanif Rangrez, a mastercraftsman belonging to the community of Neelgar or traditional indigo-dyers of Rajasthan, is the sole practitioner of *roghan* printing in Astodia (figure 19). He learnt this craft from his father and was apprenticed as an artisan at the age of 15. His father had migrated from Jaipur and set up his workshop in Ahmedabad. He employed two artisans and would print on a commission basis. He would get orders from the bazaar or customers would commission him to print yardage for garments for festivals or to be worn especially during weddings. The *sunhera* or gold-foil print (or gold dust) became popular for making garments to be worn during weddings. Earlier people offered a *chadar* that was printed with *roghan* at a dargah or to cover the tomb. Today, Hanifbhai's business relies on festival orders for *chaniya-choli* – a gathered skirt-and-blouse ensemble popular during the festivities of Navratri and Divali. The use of *roghan*-printed fabrics during Id celebrations has long been replaced by synthetic fabrics and screenprinted textiles.

The technique is a variant of wood-blockprinting. It uses a brass metal box that has a surface with a stencil of the pattern. The *roghan* is filled in the box and a wooden plunger is used that forces out the *roghan* through the brass stencil and encrusts it on the fabric's surface (figures 20 and 21). While it is wet, it is dusted with gold or silver dust and the surface is brushed to remove the excess. The fabric is lifted carefully from the table and dried in the sun. The printer's palette consists of real gold foil and real silver foil, followed

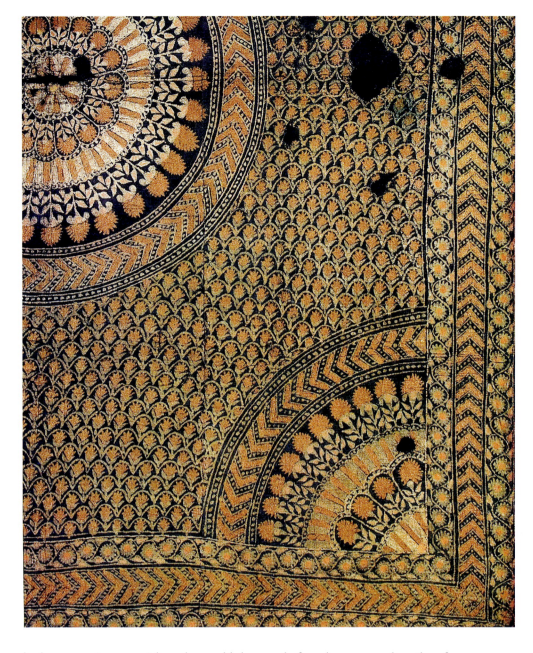

18
A 19th-century *chandarvo* or canopy that was stencil-printed with mica powder and gold and decorated with *roghan*. Powdered mica is used for silver, powdered gold and orange mixed with *roghan* have been applied on an indigo-dyed fabric. Shown here is one quarter of the canopy. From the collection of the Calico Museum of Textiles. Photograph courtesy Calico Museum of Textiles.

by less expensive materials such as gold dust made from bronze powder; silver from aluminium powder; copper powder; tinsel or glitter; flock or fibre dust. White and different coloured powders are also mixed with the *roghan* and printed.

The *roghan* printer's repertoire consists of *bel* or a stylized creeper (figure 22), a stripe or border, *buti* or small floral motif, *buta* or large motif, and *jal* or a non-directional net. The motifs are stylized forms of leaves and flowers that have been rendered suitably for the method of printing, such that the stencilled form does not cause the *roghan* to spread. They resemble motifs rendered in silk- and zari-woven brocaded textiles. Most of the designs are 40 years old as there has not been a business opportunity for the craftsman to order new blocks. Hanifbhai works with traditional *roghan* printing but does screenprinting as well, and strikes a balance between the old and the new. He venerates the traditional craft of *roghan* printing and applies his innovative mind to respond to technical challenges faced while printing on new materials and for new contexts. The main encouragement for his craft has come from design-led firms in Jaipur and Delhi and recently a collaboration with a Bangalore-based design firm to explore *roghan* with flock printed on plywood. Although located in Ahmedabad, the craftsman's local business has required him to outsource the

19
Hanif Rangrez, Khatum Bibi Rangrez, and their eldest son Feroze Rangrez in their house in Astodia. Photograph: Aratrik Dev Varman.

20
Stencils of butas or large motifs have been made on the faces of brass boxes which form the blocks for *roghan* printing. Photograph: Aratrik Dev Varman.

21
Each hollow block has a wooden plunger which forces the *roghan* or adhesive residue through the stencil. Photograph: Aratrik Dev Varman.

22
Brass blocks for borders used in *roghan* printing. A border called a *bel* is a stylized creeper or a floral stripe. Photograph: Aratrik Dev Varman.

HAND-BLOCKPRINTED TEXTILES | **119**

roghan from Azamgarh in Uttar Pradesh and the brass blocks from Jaipur. He has orders for prints from clients outside Ahmedabad. Thus, he has been part of the process of globalization and outsourcing of skills that has helped him achieve a sustained market for his traditional livelihood and a better quality of life for his family.

Mata ni Pachedi
Besides the secular traditions of blockprinting, Ahmedabad was known for Mata ni Pachedi, the handpainted and blockprinted cloths for the worship of the Mother Goddess. The Vaghari craftsmen and women who make them are known as Chitara or imagemakers, and a few families living in Vasna and Shahpur areas of Ahmedabad practise this craft today. This long, horizontal pictorial cloth has the epic of the Mata or Mother Goddess. She is depicted in all her various incarnations and occupies a prominent space in the centre surrounded by smaller figures of gods, mythological characters, animals, *malin* or women with offerings of flowers, *paniharin* or women carrying offerings in pots. All these figures were carved as blocks in Pethapur. The *pachedi* is placed behind the shrine in a temple and also used to form the walls of a temporary shelter with a *chandarvo* or canopy (see figure 18). The *pachedi* involved both techniques of handpainting and blockprinting, using natural dyes to obtain red and black.

Revival and Innovation
The blockprinting tradition of Ahmedabad has faced severe competition from the mills and the mechanized printing industry here. Between 1953 and 1957, the number of hand-blockprinters had fallen from 8,000 to 2,500 and half of these were women.[12] A revival of the blockprinting craft would impact all the skill-sets engaged in this creative industry. Design development could infuse a new life into this tradition and enable the varied artisans to earn a better livelihood. The Black & White or *Patri* Collection developed by Archana Shah illustrates how a dormant printing technique can be brought alive through

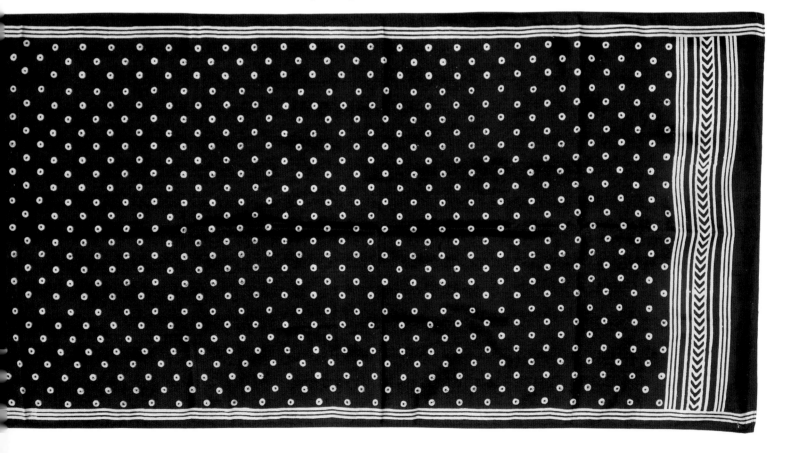

23
Silk dupatta printed by the discharge technique. Black & White Collection designed by Archana Shah and launched in her store Bandhej in 1985. Photograph: M.P. Ranjan.

24
Cotton stole printed by the *patri* technique. Black & White Collection designed and produced by Archana Shah for Bandhej in 1985. Photograph: M.P. Ranjan.

25
Silk sari printed by the *patri* technique. Black & White Collection designed by Archana Shah and launched in her store Bandhej in 1985. Photograph: M.P. Ranjan.

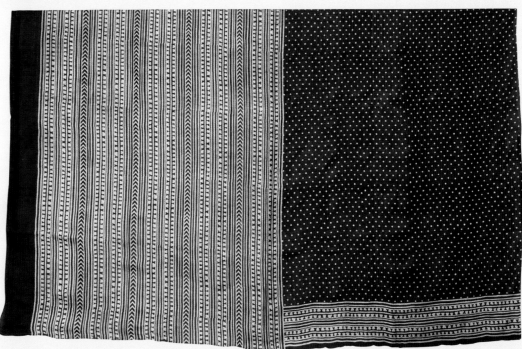

imagination and design. Archana Shah is a textile designer based in Ahmedabad who has dynamic interest in art, culture, cinema, design, and especially in the development issues of craftspersons in Gujarat. Her sensibility is informed by the textile traditions of India. Her lifestyle store called Bandhej is testimony to her close bonds with the craft traditions of India. Her explorations of the traditional technique of making a rich black colour from *patri* excited her and she creatively interpreted the technique of printing black with chemicals to develop a very successful Black & White Collection during the late 1980s and early 1990s. Her desire for a simple, uncluttered surface design led her to use basic elements like line, dot, square, and triangle to create a whole line of cotton printed products like saris, dupattas, stoles, and garments (figures 23–25).

Patri (literally flakes) refers to the use of chemicals to obtain a strong black colour in blockprinting. The traditional method of making natural black colour from iron filings and jaggery was replaced by the use of chemicals – a mixture of aniline black, potassium sulphate, and copper sulphate. The cloth was dipped in this solution and printed immediately in the wet condition with lime and gum. The lime discharged or removed the black colour and after being dried for 12 hours the fabric had to be neutralized in soda ash solution and washed several times and dried. This lengthy and immediate processing was necessary to stop the chemicals from corroding the fabric, which discouraged the printers, and the use of *patri* black declined. It is also known as *chuna patri* due to the use of lime as a discharging agent. However, Archana Shah had always appreciated the depth of colour achieved in the resist-dyeing process done in Kutch and now had found her way of celebrating the "purity of black and white" and the graphic quality of their contrast to create a contemporary expression. She responded creatively to the technique of printing and thus added a new layer to the textile tradition.

For centuries the Sabarmati river was the lifeline for blockprinters and dyers, when there were both local and distant markets for their skills. Today a few hand-blockprinters bravely continue, despite the fierce competition from new technologies of patterning textiles and changes in the market, to try and create their niche in the large middle-income home market. In the 1960s, Fakruddin Chhipa endured much hardship but had the vision to develop blockprinting on cotton fabrics using an alizarin red and natural black palette. He nurtured the tradition in his sons Faruk and Sajid Chhipa who have a well organized and tidy blockprinting workshop in Dani Limda, on the eastern bank of the Sabarmati. They have developed a system for washing and processing their grey and printed fabrics in a series of four cascading cement tanks which simulate the flowing waters of the Sabarmati river. The printed fabrics are washed first in the lowest tank and then successively in each of the tanks leading up to the tank on the highest level which signals the final wash. The printers refer to this system as the ghat or steps leading to the waterfront and several processing houses in the city offer this service (figure 26).

All these narratives – of the blockmakers of Pethapur, the Chhipas or blockprinters, the Chitaras or painters, the unsung traders and entrepreneurs like Ahmed Gamthiwala, the dyers and washermen – suggest that blockprinting could be a sustainable craft and a creative industry of the future which requires the collaboration of designers and textile technologists to make it relevant to contemporary needs and culture.

Notes
1 R.K. Trivedi, *Census 1961 Gujarat, Ahmedabad District*, Government of India, p. 54.
2 Yatin Pandya, *The Ahmedabad Chronicle: Imprints of a Millennium*, Ahmedabad: Vastu Shilpa Foundation for Studies and Research in Environmental Design, 2002.
3 Alfred Buhler and Eberhard Fischer, *Clamp Resist Dyeing of Fabrics*, Ahmedabad: Calico Museum of Textiles, 1977, p. 4.
4 Martand Singh (ed.), *Tradition and Beyond: Handcrafted Indian Textiles*, New Delhi: Roli Books, 2000, p. 84.

26
The cascading system for washing printed textiles set up at Fakruddin Blockprinters in Dani Limda. Photograph courtesy Gaatha.

5   As related by Jayanti Naik, sculptor and ceramic designer.
6   John Irwin and P.R. Schwartz, *Studies in Indo-European Textile History*, Ahmedabad: Calico Museum of Textiles, 1966, p. 16.
7   Jyotindra Jain, "Saudagiri Prints: Textiles for Far off Siam", *India Magazine*, October, 1985.
8   Nitya Amarnath and Munmun Meenakshi, "Pethapur: An Experience with Block Making", unpublished craft document, Ahmedabad: National Institute of Design, 2002.
9   Jain 1985.
10 As mentioned in http://www.chhipajamat.org.
11 As recounted by Ahmedbhai Gamthiwala, an enlightened trader and developer of blockprinted fabrics in Ahmedabad, who related his visits to Chhipawad when he was 12. After attending school he was required to help in his father's shop. This made him interested in blockprinting and he visited all the *chhipa*s' homes during the 1960s. Ahmedbhai Gamthiwala is an important resource person for blockprinted textiles of Gujarat and Rajasthan. His ancestral shops near the heritage monuments of Rani no Hajiro and Badshah no Hajiro in the Manek Chowk area of the walled city in Ahmedabad, sell a wide variety of blockprinted and screenprinted fabrics. His shop is the initiative of his father Noormohammed Haji Abdul Rahim Gamthiwala. Ahmedbhai has given marketing support to many craftspeople in Gujarat and Rajasthan by using principles of effective marketing.
12 L.C. Jain and Rita Kapadia, "Hand-Printing is Dying: Impact of Indiscriminate Mechanisation", *Economic and Political Weekly*, Vol. 19, No. 11, March 17, 1984, p. 459.

Further Reading
Bhatt, Anupama, Swasti Singh, and Diana Irani, "The Dynamics of the Craft/Consumer Relationship (Textiles of Gujarat)", unpublished craft document, Ahmedabad: National Institute of Design, 1997.
Irwin, John, *Indian Painted and Printed Fabrics*, Ahmedabad: Calico Museum of Textiles, 1970.
Nambiar, Anuradha, *Blockmakers of Pethapur, A Project by Craft Revival Trust* (unpublished), New Delhi: Craft Revival Trust, 2010.
Schwartz, Paul R., *Printing on Cotton at Ahmedabad, India in 1678*, Ahmedabad: Calico Museum of Textiles, 1970.
Shah, Angana, "Dabu Printing of Ahmedabad", unpublished craft document, National Institute of Design, 1978.
Shah, Rajdeep, "Blockprinting at Ahmedabad", unpublished craft document, National Institute of Design, 1978.

Paper, *Chopda*s, Kites
Crafting Hindu-Muslim Symbiosis

Suchitra Balasubrahmanyan

Much of the early architecture in Ahmedabad, of the 15th and 16th centuries, reflects a synthesis of Jain, Hindu, and Islamic building techniques, forms, and ornamentation. This synthesis took place against the backdrop of the often iconoclastic attitudes of the Gujarat Sultans, and these seemingly contradictory processes of conflict and coexistence continue to this day. The friction between Ahmedabad's Hindu and Muslim citizens is an undeniable blemish on the city's fair face; equally indubitable is the fact that the two communities come together in symbiotic economic and social relationships. Nowhere is this more apparent than in the field of handcrafts and this essay looks at two of them – the manufacture of traditional books of accounts and the fabrication of kites. Both are handcrafted products made from paper, a material manufactured in Ahmedabad since the early 17th century; in both crafts, Hindus and Muslims are knit together as producers and consumers.

Paper
The earliest reference to paper manufacture in Ahmedabad occurs in the East India Company records in 1619. It indicates that paper was one of the items exported from Ahmedabad to Persia.[1] This suggests that the papermaking skill must have existed even earlier.[2] In the late 17th century, frequent mention of the trade between Bombay and Surat is found in reports of the English Factories in India with a reference to a demand from Bombay for paper produced in Ahmedabad.[3] The first glimpse of the superior quality of Ahmedabadi paper appears in the *Mirat-i-Ahmadi*, a Persian history of Gujarat written in 1760:

> Although Daulatabadi and Kashmiri paper is of good glaze and texture yet it cannot be compared in whiteness to paper of Ahmedabad. There are different varieties of it. This region is sandy. So sand-grains get into its leaven and come out of it at the time of rubbing it with shell leaving invisible holes in it. It is its defect. On account of its white colour, it is taken annually to different parts of India, Arabia, and Turkey like gold.[4]

But it is in the mid-19th century that we get an idea of how paper was manufactured in the city. A young English merchant-adventurer, H.G. Briggs, visited Ahmedabad in 1848 and left this account:

We now took our way to the Shapur Darwaza, and prior to entering the city went over to the paper manufactory of a joint stock association of a Musalman – called *Kagdis*…. The article manufactured is of rather a primitive feature, but is strong and glazed, resembling similar material manipulated in Persia and the North West provinces of India. From a thousand to fifteen hundred heads are daily employed in saturating the bleached and putrescent Bengal Hemp, *ganni* thread &c., with which at a subsequent stage is mixed a quantity of wheat starch; the gelatinous mass is then received upon a close matting drawn upon a frame…. Sheet after sheet is thus taken off at the rate of forty an hour…. Upon being dried, the paper is removed and undergoes the operation of receiving that highly glazed appearance, which it possesses, by a marble roller being smartly drawn over an angular concave surface. Five descriptions of paper are thus made of various sizes, strength and lustre; the most inferior is the *Barigiora*, sold between two and three annas a quire, while the *Saib khani*, which is the first quality, realises between twenty to twenty-four annas per quire; the intermediate descriptions are called Mahmud Shahai, Murad Shahai and Kambati.[5]

Paper is no longer manufactured in Ahmedabad but vestiges of the craft live on in the manufacture of the *deshi nama chopda* or traditional books of accounts in which merchants and traders maintain records of financial transactions.

Deshi Nama Chopda or Books of Accounts

Every year in October–November on Dhan Teras, two days before the festival of Divali, the merchants, traders, and manufacturers of western India perform a ritual to open their new *deshi nama chopda*s (usually referred to as *chopda*) or books of accounts. On Divali, an invocation is made to Lakshmi, the goddess of wealth, and the final entries are made on the old books of accounts, thus closing the financial year. The next day, which is celebrated as New Year and marks the start of the next business year, the new books of accounts are ritually inaugurated with one symbolic financial transaction and then put away; regular business then begins on the fifth day of the new year.

Since Ahmedabadis are a predominantly mercantile society with a long history of subcontinental and transcontinental trade involving complex financial transactions, the

1
A view of Kagdi Soniwala's shop which has been selling *deshi nama chopda*s for four generations. Photograph: Hansil Dabhi.

*chopda*s come in various shapes and sizes for different accounting tasks. These books of accounts are primarily manufactured and sold by the Muslim Kagdi community, which earlier manufactured paper, and this continuity can be observed in the names of the different types of account books as we shall soon see (figure 1).

Covers and Binding

*Deshi nama chopda*s have a distinctive appearance, with covers in the auspicious bright red. Earlier the covers, *puttha*, were made of deep red leather but as it became more expensive, it was replaced with cardboard. In the books seen today, cardboard is covered with red cloth, with a thin sheet of sponge inserted between the two for padding, and overstitched by machine in zigzag pattern in white thread, giving the cover strength as well as its distinctive look. The zigzag pattern is not random – it has a visually clear point where the stitching starts and another where it ends. When the cover is folded over the pages, the ending stitch goes on the back cover. Thus, though both sides of the cover might look the same to the uninitiated eye, there are definite front and back sides which have to be honoured when the book is used. The covers are made by a group of craftsmen called *putthawala*s. Today, many families in diverse occupations still carry this name as a surname, indicating that at some time in the past they must have been engaged in making book covers.

2
Large *chopda*s with pages crimped into eight columns for accounting purposes. Photograph: Hansil Dabhi.

The largest of the *chopda*s are the Sahibkhani group, which are usually long, horizontal volumes with the inner pages crimped into eight columns, four for recording debit transactions and four for credit transactions (figure 2). The largest is usually of 21 centimetres height and 69 centimetres length with the crimps running along the length. The next set of large books are the Muradshahi, which also have eight-column crimps; the largest of these is usually 17 by 53 centimetres. There are also the eight-column Vara for taking creditors' signatures on payment of money, the 12-column Barasal for recording petty cash transactions, and the eight-column Khambati for day-to-day cash transactions. The *oliya* or *ublak* books are used by moneylenders to record rough notes immediately after a transaction has taken place, which are then transferred into the main account books. As can be seen from the names of the books, many of them are the same as the varieties of paper manufactured in Ahmedabad described by Briggs. Each of these specialized groups of books was probably made from the paper of that name and though the paper has now been replaced by mill-manufactured paper from different parts of India, the names continue and refer to the type of account books instead.

3
*Chopda*s with *bichche* binding.
Photograph: Hansil Dabhi.

4
A *mathhe*-bound *chopda* with a view of a page crimped in eight columns for accounting purposes.
Photograph: Hansil Dabhi.

5
Mathhe-bound and *apa silai chopda*s ready for the next accounting year. Photograph: Hansil Dabhi.

*Chopda*s are bound in different ways. In *bichche* (centre) binding, sheets are folded down the middle and stitched at the centre along the fold, and the binding string is visible along the spine (figure 3). Another form of the same kind of centre-stitching is called "book". In *mathhe* (top) binding, the sheets are not folded but gathered and stitched along one, usually the shorter, edge with extra strips of fabric for support (figure 4). *Mathhe*-bound books are usually folded in half with the lower cardboard cover curling over to support the unbound side for protection (see figure 2). The third popular form of binding is referred to as *apa silai* where folios are gathered into sets and several sets are stitched together along the spine. The individual sets are stitched by women, giving rise to the name of this form of binding where *apa* is Urdu for older sister and *silai* means stitching. The thickness of books is measured in *gha* which refers to 144 pages, or *ani* which refers to nine pages. Books of different thicknesses have multiples or fractions of *gha* and *ani*. Thus a book of 288 pages is *bey* (two) *gha* and a book of 54 pages would be called *chha* (six) *ani*. Regardless of type of binding or thickness, most books are secured with a twine which is wound round and tucked in to keep them from opening up (figure 5). As the books get larger and the number of pages increases, the twine gets thicker to secure the book safely. *Chopda* binding is primarily done by the menfolk of the Kagdi community, except for the *apa silai*.

Hindu-Muslim Symbiosis

As business is so central to Ahmedabadi life, the rituals around the account books are many and they knit Hindu and Muslim communities in interesting ways. The Muslim Kagdis confer with Hindu astrologers and draw up a table of auspicious dates and times in the day – the most favourable time to place orders for account books with Kagdis, the propitious time to collect the books from the shop, the most auspicious time to ritually inaugurate the books by inscribing the name of Goddess Lakshmi, and the most favourable time to restart business five days after Divali. This timetable of days, dates, and times is printed and delivered by the Kagdis to their Hindu and Jain customers (figure 6). Most merchants and businessmen buy their books from particular Kagdis and it is not uncommon to find a manufacturer-customer relationship which goes back several generations in both a Kagdi's family and his customer's. The books which have been ordered are wrapped in red cloth and handed over at the auspicious moment. Often the customer will insist on receiving the package from the hands of a particular member of the

6
Calendar of auspicious days for ordering and inaugurating account books, distributed by Kagdi Soniwala to his customers. Photograph: Suchitra Balasubrahmanyan.

Kagdi family whom he regards as a person who brings luck. Today, the *deshi nama chopda* is rapidly being replaced by the computer and the government has made the accounting year uniform all over the country, starting in April. Yet, the Divali rituals continue, taking on a symbolic form. A few account books are inaugurated as of old and the computer is included in the worship.

Apart from businessmen and merchants, another community for which Kagdis make books are the *barot*s or traditional genealogists of Hindu communities. In an oral culture where very few people were literate, *barot*s played an important role in recording births, marriages, deaths, and other significant events in people's lives. The practice continues despite the altered circumstances of modern life. Each *barot* has a fixed, multi-generational relationship with several families for whom he creates and maintains family records and keeps track of the family's genealogy. Since *barot*s maintain family registers over generations, the *barot na chopda* or *barot*'s books are among the oldest testaments to the Kagdi's skill.

Kites

Come January, kites dot the Ahmedabad skyline in preparation for the Hindu festival of Makar Sankranti, celebrated all over Gujarat as Utran. The word is the local version of the Sanskrit Uttarayan which refers to the start of the sun's northward journey and its transition into the zodiac sign Makar or Capricorn. The festival falls on January 14 each year and while the occasion has a Hindu conception, kiteflying on this day brings the city together as men and women, young and old, unmindful of religious or caste affiliation, engage in exuberant, sometimes fiercely competitive, kiteflying.

The Antiquity of Kiteflying

Makar Sankranti is a major winter festival in India, though Gujarat and Rajasthan are the only regions where kites are flown on this day (apart from Mumbai which has a significant Gujarati population). It is difficult to say why kites are flown on Utran, or to gauge the antiquity of the practice, as not one Arabic, Persian, Hindu, or Jain manuscript makes any reference to it. Even those texts which give extensive details about Ahmedabad are silent on this. The only allusion we have is from a legend. It is said that Saint Shah Alam, a revered Sufi saint of Ahmedabad in the mid-15th century, once came upon a group of young boys playing truant from school and flying kites. "This is not the time to fly kites," he admonished them, "but the time to pay attention to your studies." The story suggests that kiteflying was prevalent as a sport in 15th-century Ahmedabad and is likely to have existed even prior to this period.[6]

7
A view of the old city on Makar Sankranti. Photograph: Surendra Patel, courtesy Kite Museum.

The answer to the question of how kitemaking and kiteflying came to be associated with such a major festival in Ahmedabad lies in the realm of speculation. Kiteflying in the spring season of Basant is popular in the northwestern parts of the subcontinent where the pleasant weather and gentle winds make it an ideal season for the sport. Afghanistan has a vibrant tradition of kiteflying at this time, as does Lahore, and both places are well known for aggressive kitefighting competitions. Historical references and miniature paintings suggest that the Mughals were kiteflying enthusiasts as were the kings and nobles of Rajasthan.[7] The cities and towns of Rajasthan also fly kites on Makar Sankranti and even today the area has very skilled kitemakers. It is probable that large-scale kiteflying in the pre-spring season in Ahmedabad originated after the late 16th century when Gujarat was annexed to the Mughal empire, and strengthened in the period that followed when Rajasthani nobles appointed by the emperor administered the province. Kiteflying was also widespread in Uttar Pradesh and this region became connected with Gujarat as Krishna worship spread to Gujarat after the 16th century. A glance at the craft of kitemaking as it is today offers some insight into how these diverse strands come together to make kiteflying such a major festival in Ahmedabad (figure 7).

The Craft of Kitemaking in Ahmedabad

The subcontinent converges in the city to prepare for the kiteflying festival. The paper comes from mills in Maharashtra and the South, the string is locally produced, the bamboo comes from the Northeast, and the craftsmen from the North. Around late August every year, Muslim craftsmen from Jaipur, Jodhpur, and Bikaner in Rajasthan, from Agra, Mathura, Rampur, Bareilly, and Lucknow in Uttar Pradesh, and from Delhi migrate to Ahmedabad to start making kites for Utran. Many of them move from

8
Cut kite papers. Photograph: Kunal Panchal.

9 and 10
Inside a kitemaking *karkhana*.
Photographs: Arvind Caulagi.

one region to another through the year as different parts of India fly kites on different occasions. For example, the kiteflying season in Uttar Pradesh is during the Raksha Bandhan festival in July–August and in Delhi on Independence Day in August. So craftsmen come from these places after the kiteflying seasons are over, to make kites for Utran in Gujarat and Rajasthan. There are local craftsmen too, living in the Jamalpur and Dani Limda areas of Ahmedabad, but most of them report that their ancestors came from Rajasthan or Uttar Pradesh. Craftsmen from Uttar Pradesh believe that the patron saint of kitemakers is Hakim Lukman who they say was the first person to make and fly kites in Mughal times. Whether Lukman was a historical or mythical figure is not clear, but his location in the Mughal period suggests that the making and flying of kites received encouragement at this time.

Craftsmen report that earlier all the stages of kitemaking – cutting and pasting the paper, preparing the *daddho* (vertical bamboo spine) and *kamaan* (bow-shaped bamboo spar that holds the paper with the required tension), making the *dori* (string frame along the four sides) and the *gullo* (triangular tail-piece which balances the kite) or *phumta* (plumed tail), and assembling the kite – were done at one location by a single group of people. Now kites are made in an assembly line where each stage is completed at a different location (figures 8–10). Craftsmen from different regions specialize in different kinds of kites and have expertise in different designs. For example, craftsmen from Uttar Pradesh make good *lakdedar* kites in a checkered pattern. The local Jamalpur *karigar*s or craftsmen are specialists in the *kathdar* geometrical designs. Specialists in cutting designs in paper have preferred skill areas – some cut only geometrical designs, others specialize in designs which involve curvilinear cutting. Cutting paper for kites is a highly skilled task specially when a design involves many components of varying shapes and colours. The overlap allowance for gluing is a mere 1/16th of an inch (0.15 centimetre) and to make an intricate pattern that is well balanced for flying is an art based in science. The *manjha* or string for the kites is prepared by other experts. They use string from local spinning mills on which a coating of coloured glue and ground glass is applied to enhance its ability to cut another string (figures 11 and 12).

Kites come in many shapes: rocket (longer than broad), *cheel* (broader than long), *gol* (round); and in different sizes: *dodh tav, adhi tav, chartav, pavlo, genshiyo, at*, the full-size

11
Preparation of *manjha* with a mixture of gum, glass powder, and colour. Photograph: Arvind Caulagi.

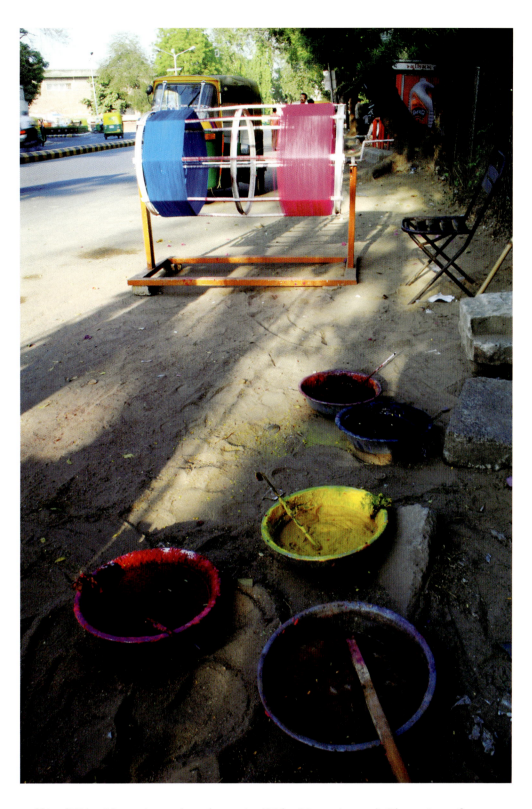

12
Preparation of different coloured *manjha* in the street. Photograph: Kunal Panchal.

ankhiyo (27 by 30 centimetres), and *pauniyo* (20 by 30 centimetres). The variety of patterns is vast: *tipatti* (three-stripes), *tiri* (arrow-shape), *do ankhi* (two eyes), *chand-tara* (crescent moon and star), *gaind-dar* (round motif), *lahariya* (wave pattern), *pandar* (heart-shaped leaf motif), *karondia* (two halves on either side of the spine in different colours), *nakhuniya* (inverted crescent resembling a fingernail above the spar), and many more (figures 13a–d). Kites in plain colours have their own names like the red *dulhan* (bride), the yellow *basanti*, the purple *baingan* (aubergine), blue *asmani* (sky), and the black *habshi* (Ethiopian). The main kite bazaar was in the Tankshal area in the heart of the walled core of Ahmedabad

13a–d
Decorative kites. Photographs: Bhanu Shah, courtesy Kite Museum.

where the Mint was originally located. The market has now shifted north to Raipur with other markets coming up to serve kiteflyers in the expanding city (figures 14–17).

Miniature kites are specially prepared on Utran, ranging from about 3 centimetres square to about 6 centimetres square, faithful in every detail – bamboo supports, multicoloured designs, with miniature tails and plumes and trims of shiny golden paper. These are prepared not for actual flying but to offer to the baby Krishna worshipped by the Vaishnavas. On the morning of Utran these tiny kites along with miniature *phirki*s (spools for kite string) are offered to the infant god for his enjoyment in Vaishnava temples and shrines all over the city (figure 18). In home shrines, the idol along with the miniature kite and *phirki* is carried out into the open so that the child god can fly his kite symbolically and enjoy the sight of the sky dotted with kites. Even on occasions of intense communal friction, the Muslim craftsmen ensure that the divine baby is not denied this annual pleasure.

14 (opposite)
Inside view of an old kite shop with a photograph of the founder. Photograph: Arvind Caulagi.

15 (opposite)
View of kite shops selling various types of kites during the Kite Festival. Photograph: Arvind Caulagi.

136   Suchitra Balasubrahmanyan

PAPER, *CHOPDAS*, KITES | 137

A few days after Utran all the migrant families collect their money from the kite traders and leave, either to return to their home villages or to prepare for the next kiteflying day in another part of the country. A few months later, with the approach of summer, the Kagdis begin preparations to produce *deshi nama chopda*s for the approaching new business year.

Thus, two paper products, *deshi nama chopda*s and kites, have knit the communities of Ahmedabad over the last 500 years, bringing together craft, ritual, and sheer enjoyment – despite unfortunate periods of discord and disharmony.

16
A woman with a cart of kites in the street. Photograph: Kunal Panchal.

17
A view of a *phirki* shop during the Kite Festival. Photograph: Arvind Caulagi.

18
Kites offered to baby Krishna in a private Vaishnava temple on Makar Sankranti. Photograph: Suchitra Balasubrahmanyan.

Acknowledgements
I would like to thank Bhanu Shah, Chintan Pandya, Ashok Shrimali, Muhammad Habib Soniwala, and Mitan Parekh for their help in gathering material for this essay.

Notes
1. Makrand Mehta, *Indian Merchants and Entrepreneurs in Historical Perspective*, Delhi: Academic Foundation, 1991, p. 117.
2. In the middle of the 15th century, late in the reign of Sultan Ahmed Shah, a momentous transformation occurred in Jain scholarship as palm leaves were replaced by paper. The reasons for this are not clear, but at one go, palm-leaf manuscripts in the famous Jain *bhandar*s (repositories for manuscripts on religious and secular subjects) of Gujarat and Rajasthan were copied on paper. Such a large-scale shift from palm-leaf suggests that a ready source of paper was close at hand, possibly in Ahmedabad. Rasiklal Parikh and Hariprasad Shastri (eds.), *Gujaratno Rajkiya ane Sanskrutik Itihas*, Vol. 5: *Sultanate Kaal*, Ahmedabad: Sheth Bholabhai Jeshingbhai Adhyayan-Sanshodhan Vidyabhavan, 1977, p. 369.
3. Surendra Gopal, *Commerce and Crafts in Gujarat: 16th and 17th Centuries*, New Delhi: People's Publishing House, 1975, p. 101.
4. Ali Muhammad Khan and, M.F. Lokhandwala (trans.), *Mirat-i-Ahmadi*, Baroda: Oriental Institute, M.S. University, 1965, p. 12.
5. H.G. Briggs, *Cities of Gujarashtra: Their Topography and History Illustrated in the Journal of A Recent Tour*, Bombay: Times Press, 1849, pp. 266–67.
6. Personal conversation with Bhanu Shah, expert on the history of kites and creator of Ahmedabad's Kite Museum, December 12, 2010.
7. M.P. Srivastava, *Social Life under the Great Mughals, 1526–1700 A.D.*, Allahabad: Chugh Publications, p. 43; Harbans Mukhia, *The Mughals of India*, New Delhi: Wiley India, 2009, p. 97. The Kite Museum in Ahmedabad shows kiteflying scenes in miniature paintings of the Mewar school of the early 18th century, and from Kota, Bikaner, and Jaipur of the late 18th and 19th centuries.

Ahmedabad 600
Readings from the Palimpsest

Yatin Pandya

The City is like a palimpsest. Many have traversed its sands, and some footprints have transcended the overlays of time. Manuscripts, paintings, etchings, photographs, and even folklore serve as hieroglyphics, which unveil the City's persona over time. On the 600th anniversary of the establishment of Ahmedabad, this is a small attempt to decipher the hieroglyphics on its sands. These serve as clues for us to traverse further on the path. We take an interpreted look at them to learn the lessons from the City's scroll, to infer from its initiatives, to savour its spirit, to take pride in its people, to debate its development directions, and to invigorate its visions.

The City in Travel Sketches and Photographs
Dutch traveller Philip Baldaeus's account in 1672 is one of the most comprehensive overviews of Ahmedabad's cityscape and the prevailing context. As observed in the sketch, echoing Emperor Jahangir's observation of it as a "city of dust", Ahmedabad seems to stand amidst a desert where camels ply and date palms dot the landscape. The skyline of the fortified city is characterized by the rising spires of its mosques.

Such paintings also provide the clues to connect the dots in the puzzles of time. For example, the arched, intricately carved, stone *jali* of the Sidi Saiyyad mosque (1573) depicting date palms has by default come to be the associable symbol of the city (figure 1). How is it that it depicts date palm trees which are no longer found locally? Baldaeus's account answers the question by stating these to be the indigenous species then. Similarly James Forbes' etchings of 1781 depict the existence of towering spires of the Jami mosque which fell prey to an earthquake soon after.

Colonel Biggs' photographs of the 19th century are some of the most conclusive documents depicting the physical state of the city's monuments and the built environment in general. For example, his photograph of the city wall shows it in its restored state which verifies the critical anecdote related below, that speaks volumes for citizens' initiatives in city affairs.

Citizens' Initiatives
Ahmedabad successfully pioneered a model of local self-governance, as early as 1833. By the exertion of English administrators, much interest was generated in the restoration of the fort walls built way back in 1429 by Mahmud Begada. The traders and merchants of the city voluntarily raised a fund, called the "City Walls Restoration Fund", through a levy

1
Stone *jali* of the Sidi Saiyyad mosque.

on the sale of ghee (clarified butter). The Fund was administered by a committee consisting of the city judge, the collector, and two citizens. Not only were the city walls effectively restored with this Fund, but seeing its success, the subscribers to the Fund continued to contribute to and expand the Fund for the general management and improvement of the city. Revenue through this Fund was made available to Ahmedabad Municipality for almost 50 years. This probably is the earliest example of organized municipal self-government in the country.

The spirit of the city as the chemistry of the collective got crystallized in the form of the *mahajan*s or guilds. These assumed powers which could not be challenged either by the courts or by the government bureaucracy. They functioned in the interest of the collective good and public well-being. It was the *mahajan*s who took business orders and distributed these to their members to ensure equality as well as prevent undue competition and disparity of income amongst them. Workers' wages, minimum base price, dealing with outstation traders, offering verdicts on any trade-related disputes, ensuring amity between communities, introduction of taxes, representation to authorities, and initiation and management of charitable activities were all within the purview of the *mahajan*s. They were involved with philanthropic activities as well. The imposition of a quarter per cent octroi to compensate the Nagarsheth family who had saved the city by paying ransom money to the Marathas, the imposition of a surcharge on ghee to collect funds for repairs of city walls, the creation of a *panjarapol* (asylum for infirm animals), the installation and maintenance of *parabadi*s (bird feeders) are some of the profound examples of the social and charitable work undertaken by the *mahajan*s.

Ahmedabad was arguably the only Indian city modernizing on its own terms. Reliant neither on the patronage of court, monarch, or colonial power, nor on the exploitation of the surrounding countryside, Ahmedabad has had a long history of self-generating prosperity through its trade, commerce, and textile manufacturing (figure 2). It has shown considerable independence in the management of its affairs even though it was never a city-state.

Ahmedabad turned its mercantile wealth into industrial success when Ranchhodlal Chhotalal founded the first textile mill in the city against all possible odds. It was an act of sheer personal will and determination of an individual, which morphed the city into an industrial giant. Born in a brahmin family in Ahmedabad, Ranchhodlal first dreamt of the idea of setting up a textile mill in India as early as 1847. Ahmedabad was not a port. It did not have the humid climate suitable for growing cotton. All the machinery for a textile mill had to be imported from England, competition from European textile mills was tough, and the tax structure adverse. There was no railway and no coal mines nearby. Despite such adversities Ranchhodlal imported machinery from England through Dadabhai Naoroji. On the first occasion the machinery sank in the low seas, and its engineer died of cholera. It was reordered, unloaded at the bay of Cambay (Khambhat), and from there brought to Ahmedabad in bullock-carts. The mill, named Ahmedabad Spinning and Weaving Co. Ltd. (Shahpur Mill), became operational from May 30, 1861 with an investment of one lakh rupees. The rest is history. Ahmedabad, in less than a few decades, came to be recognized as the Manchester of the East, exporting cotton textiles to Europe. It is also interesting to note that the shares of all the textile mills of the city were solely subscribed by its citizens.

Ahmedabad has had a self-sustaining chain of individuals setting up industries, industries patronizing institutions, and institutions moulding a new breed of individuals. No wonder, the city prides itself in its institutional resources, be they scientific, research, educational, or philanthropic. They are acclaimed the world over for their concern and quality. Following in the footsteps of the first Nagarsheth, Sheth Shantidas Zaveri, who donated to schools as well as to archives and libraries, subsequent generations of leading citizens have been instrumental in initiating and establishing civic institutions. Harkunvar Shethani supported the first civil hospital in Ahmedabad in 1855, a girls' school, a women's training centre, as well as the Gujarat Vernacular Society. Sir Chinubhai Ranchhodlal established a technical and science college. Amritlal Hargovandas set up the commerce, arts, science, and medical colleges. Ambalal Sarabhai supported the setting up of the Ahmedabad Textile Industry's Research Association, B.M. Institute of Mental Health, Indian Institute of Management, National Institute of Design, and Jyotisangh (an organization to empower women). Kasturbhai Lalbhai set up engineering, architecture, planning, and management institutes as well as other cultural and research institutes. And Dr Vikram Sarabhai brought to the city scientific organizations such as the Space

2
Cityscape of textile mills with Kankaria Lake in the foreground, 1937, by Pranlal Patel.

Application Centre and Physical Research Laboratory in which Ahmedabad takes pride. Nirma University, set up by a foundation created by a local detergent company, is one of the recent additions to this list.

In a democratic set-up, need we be dependent on authorities to envision our city's priorities and the course of its development? Does the city have to recast itself on the whim of the authorities, the individual agendas of ministers, the fancy of commissioners, the perceived priorities of government officers, or even the personal interpretations of professionals? Can these translate into collective value and shared vision?

Architecture as a Saga of Creative Regionalism

An enterprising community with an avant-garde outlook, yet rooted to its place and traditions, is one of the unique traits of Ahmedabad. This has not only led to flourishing trade and business but a breed of architecture full of exploration and with the spirit of creative regionalism. The architectural landscape of Ahmedabad stretches across the centuries. Buildings from different eras coexist as testimony to the Indian phenomenon of adaptive assimilation. Nurtured by reveries as well as realities, the architecture has always remained an amalgamation of deep-rooted traditional values with the aspirations of changing times.

Sultanate architecture creatively fused Hindu craftsmanship, trabeated construction techniques, and local motifs with Islamic plan geometry, pointed arches, domes, and *jali*s.

3
Jami mosque. Photograph: Yatin Pandya.

4
Hutheesing temple. Photograph: Yatin Pandya.

The Jami mosque (1424, figure 3) illustrates the fact with juxtapositions of *toran kaman*s (ceremonial gateways) and *kalash* (waterpot) motifs.

The overwhelming richness of wooden elements in havelis has left its imprint even in stone monuments. The Hutheesing Jain temple (1879, figure 4) is an example of this creative regionalism through the integration of vernacular building elements such as *jharoka*s (balconies), porticos, and *chhaja*s (protective slabs) into the canonical dictates of temple architecture.

Eclecticism was inevitable but it was mature and pleasing, as newer thoughts were creatively regionalized. The tradition of combining the local with the foreign blossomed during colonial rule. British architect Claude Batley's architecture stands tall in this regard (figure 5). In the post-Independence era, the pragmatism and progressive outlook of Ahmedabad's enterprising community brought home the best of international architecture. The Swiss-French maestro Le Corbusier was bestowed with total faith and given a blank canvas to paint on (figure 6). This faith and freedom is well rewarded in four of his creations, each unique in its own way. Ahmedabad has proven to be a fertile ground for creative ideas to germinate. The cooling towers of the Ahmedabad Electricity Company (figure 7) inspired Corbusier in creating the roof form of Chandigarh's Assembly building.

The unique contribution of Louis Kahn is well known, but Ahmedabad narrowly missed on its canvas the signature of another architectural legend, Frank Lloyd Wright, who prepared a sketch design for the Calico Administrative Building (1946) which unfortunately was abandoned (figure 8). This architectural saga of constant upgradation and experimentation lives on in the works of contemporary Indian masters. A search for contextual relevance and adaptation to changing times has become the preoccupation of contemporary architects.

5
The Town Hall (designed by Gregson, Batley and King) with its environs in 1937, by Pranlal Patel.

6
Photograph of Le Corbusier explaining the concept of the museum to municipal officers on June 23, 1953, by Pranlal Patel.

7
Laying of cables across the riverbed for the erstwhile Ahmedabad Electricity Company in 1943, by Pranlal Patel.

8
Sketch for the Calico Administrative Building by Frank Lloyd Wright, 1946.

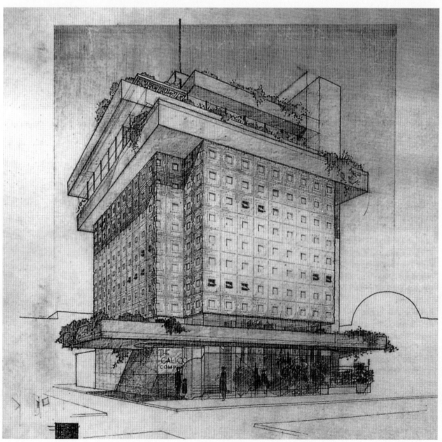

Freedom Movement: A Tale between Two Coverpages

Ahmedabad has very interesting associations with both India's colonization and its freedom. It was in Ahmedabad, while on a boating excursion in 1618, that Jahangir granted British agent Sir Thomas Roe the permission to trade. Unknowingly this turned out to be the first thread in the bonds of slavery. Exactly 200 years later in 1818, the Union Jack was flown in the city for the first time. Ahmedabad wiped out its guilt nearly 100 years later, in 1915, when Gandhi returned from South Africa and made Ahmedabad his base for the Independence movement. However even before this, Ahmedabad city's contribution to the country's freedom movement is evident. In 1857 Ahmedabad participated in the first attempt to revolt against British rule. Several soldiers of the Maratha regiment were killed in this incident. In 1876, the Swadeshi Udyogvardhak Mandali to promote indigenous industry was founded jointly by Ambalal Sakarlal Desai, Premabhai Himabhai, Ranchhodlal Chhotalal, Hargovandas Kantawala, Bechardas Lashkari, and Lalshankar Umiyashankar. The year 1902 witnessed the second Congress convention, in which Ambalal Sakarlal Desai was the chief of the welcome committee. In 1903 the Swadeshi Vastu Sahakar Mandali was founded in the city in wake of the spreading Swadeshi movement. This was the second most important step towards independence and political freedom.

In 1905, Keshavlal Mehta and Chunilal Mehta passed the proposal of Swadeshi, as a result of which 40 Bengali youths came to Ahmedabad to learn the textile trade. In exchange, they taught Ahmedabadi youth the revolutionary song "Vande Mataram" and the technique of manufacturing bombs (figure 9). On November 13, 1909, Governor-General Lord Minto escaped a bomb explosion, which was meant to kill him, just outside the Raipur Darwaza. While Ahmedabad had leaders like Mahatma Gandhi and Sardar Vallabhbhai Patel choosing to make the city their base, the freedom movement actually became a part of the city's way of life. As seen in Pranlal Patel's photographs, the *garba* festivities were centred around Gandhiji's *rentio*, spinning wheel, as the symbol of freedom (figure 10). Even the popular format of the *akhada* (space for gymnastics and physical training) along the street square was used to raise public awareness and participation.

After Gandhiji's arrival in 1915, Ahmedabad became a centre of anti-British activities (figure 11). The protest against the Rowlatt Act in 1919, in which Ahmedabadi freedom

9
The team of volunteers at United Bengal Home, Ahmedabad, in 1905. Photograph courtesy Yatin Pandya.

10
Garba around a *rentio* in 1937, by Pranlal Patel.

11
Sarojini Naidu and Gandhiji hoisting India's flag at the V.S. Hospital grounds, by Pranlal Patel.

fighters Indulal Yagnik and Jeevanlal played a major role, saw the enforcement of martial law for the first time in the city. In the 36th Congress convention Gandhiji put forward the proposal of personal and group satyagraha against the British. Students of Gujarat College went on strike, resulting in college principal Acharya Kripalani holding classes in the open.

In 1930 Mrudula Sarabhai formed a *vanarsena* or children's army (literally monkey army as in the *Ramayana*), which introduced them to the fight for freedom. In order that girl students might be prevented from singing "God Save the King", a new municipal girls' school was opened where the students were taught "Vande Mataram" instead. As a result, these girls were denied admission to college. On the very first day of the Quit India movement started by Gandhiji on August 8, 1942, Umakant Kadiya embraced martyrdom, while on the next day Vinod Kinariwala got shot while trying to hoist the Indian flag in an outbreak of riots outside Gujarat College.

In this way Ahmedabad saw many great personalities take shape during the freedom struggle. Sardar Vallabhbhai Patel's grooming in civic leadership was in Ahmedabad and he was chairman of Ahmedabad Municipality between 1924 and 1928. During his chairmanship he concentrated on fundamental civic issues of health, hygiene, public amenities, and infrastructure. To overcome the frequent outbreak of diseases he initiated a massive clean-up drive. One such move was to clean Kankaria Lake where fishes died in the polluted water lacking oxygen.

12
Weekly flea-market (*gujri*) in front of the Sidi Saiyyad mosque, 1937, by Pranlal Patel.

Ahmedabad 600

It is seldom in one's life that one gets to witness the centenary of a city. We have had this rare honour and privilege, as on February 26, 2011 the City of Ahmedabad celebrated its sixth centenary since its founding in 1411 by the Sultanate king Ahmed Shah.

Ahmedabad has been a city of living paradoxes. A lived-in-heritage, where history is still alive as tradition. Truly a city for, by, and of the people – from cooperative housing to the textile industry, from women's education and enterprise to underground drainage and piped water supply, Ahmedabad has pioneered many avant-garde concepts and set examples for the city of the future to emulate. It is with a deep sense of gratitude and pride that

13 and 14
Diverse activities along the Sabarmati: bathing during the solar eclipse of 1943; and drying of washed clothes on the riverbed. Both photographs by Pranlal Patel.

we salute the City and share the values and vitality it has imprinted in the sands of time, while also pondering over the course of development today. Images of then and now are dimensions in themselves for the ensuing debates.

Multiplexes and Malls versus Market Squares and Streets

Traditional marketplaces, being open to nature and people, are inherently and constantly changing and this also triggers spontaneous and unpredictable developments (figure 12). There is a range of activity generators for people from different age groups, diverse economic backgrounds, and various cultural underpinnings. Truly pluralistic.

Multiplexes and malls at the other end are marked by monotony, exclusivity, and passivity, and thereby in many ways by alienation. It perhaps is a case of hypocrisy versus democracy, formal versus informal, exclusive versus inclusive, and imposed versus ingrained.

Riverfront as Arena of Activity versus a Concrete-lined Canal

Ahmedabad was established on the banks of the Sabarmati or Shwabhramati as it was originally termed. The river has all along perhaps been a stretch of sand rather than a river on which the city was built. Yet, it was revered way back since its reference in the *Padmapurana* (c. 8th to 11th century), and has been a seat for sages like Dadhichi. Even Gandhiji chose to set up his ashram on the bank of the Sabarmati. The river served as civic node, an open space for collective initiatives (figures 13 and 14). Vital even without water,

it caught the fancy of many photographers including Henri Cartier-Bresson. How inclusive, diverse, democratic, and active does the contemporary channel of stagnant water, fed from the river Narmada and stored between barrages, promise to be?

Growth versus Development

The pictures of Pankornaka or Pankuvarnaka taken in the 1930s reveal the glory and riches of the city intact till the recent past (figure 15). Not only do the coordinated facade and street characterize the city, its highly ornate street lights, furnished footpath, and accessories also speak of the riches which rivalled European streets. The footwear and headgear unmistakably worn by each person also demonstrate the glory of the town and its riches enjoyed even by its common citizens.

Erased Hieroglyphics from the Palimpsest

What the City and citizens preserved for over half a millennium as an integral manifestation of its cultures and ways of life seems to be getting lost rapidly before our eyes. Delhi Darwaza, the gate leading to Delhi, which is also known as Idaria Darwaza, is one of the 12 gates of the fortified city. The three-arched gate was protected by one cannon. The gate had an upper floor as *nagarkhana* or *naubatkhana*, where drums were beaten to pronounce arrival. The photograph of the procession carrying Gandhiji's ashes through the gate in 1948 (figure 16), clearly shows the existence of the upper floor till the post-Independence period. In the absence of a legal framework to protect structures less than a century old, and perhaps the lost sense of association between citizens and such artefacts, structures like the upper floor of the Darwaza have been lost in our own lifetime. Gone is the spirit of 1833, when the sense of belonging that Ahmedabad's citizens had with the city made them voluntarily contribute to restoring its wall.

Milestones are not destinations in themselves but rather pointers of the path ahead. They become excuses to ponder and reaffirm the course of the journey. The sixth centenary of the founding of Ahmedabad city has the potential of being such a milestone. A milestone to make us ponder and envision the City's future directions.

15
Pankornaka in 1937, by Pranlal Patel.

16
The procession with Mahatma Gandhi's ashes moving through the gates and streets of Ahmedabad, 1948, by Pranlal Patel.

Acknowledgement
This article draws on the invaluable visual resource of Shri Pranlal Karamshibhai Patel, legendary photographer of Ahmedabad. Born on January 1, 1910, he has lived through two centenaries of the city and shares moments of the past century frozen through his lens. Having taken up photography in 1932, after a short stint in painting under the apprenticeship of Ravishankar Rawal, his images of the city are a substantial visual document that heightens our understanding of it. We salute Shri Pranlalbhai for his mammoth contribution, and thank him for giving us the opportunity to present some of his images here.

References
Burgess, Jas, *The Muhammadan Architecture of Ahmadabad*, London: Archaeological Survey of India (New Imperial Series), 1900.
Hope, Theodore and James Fergusson, *Architecture at Ahmedabad, the Capital of Goozerat*, London: John Murray, 1866.
Jote, Ratnamanirao Bhimrao, *Gujaratnu Patnagar: Amdavad*, Ahmedabad: Gujarat Sahitya Sabha, 1929.
Pandya, Yatin, *The Ahmedabad Chronicle: Imprints of a Millennium*, Ahmedabad: Vastu Shilpa Foundation for Studies and Research in Environmental Design, 2002.
Soundara Rajan, K.V., *Ahmadabad*, New Delhi: Director General, Archaeological Survey of India, 1980.

Index

Page numbers in **bold** indicate captions

Abdur Rahim Khan-i-Khanan 52
Abhikram 77, 78
Abul Fazl 10, 58
Abuwala, Sheikhadam 15
Adalaj Vav 28
Afghanistan 132
Agra 132
Ahmedabad Education Society 66
Ahmedabad Electricity Company 145, **147**
Ahmedabad Municipality 142, 150
Ahmedabad Spinning and Weaving Co. Ltd/Shahpur Mill 143
Ahmedabad Textile Industry's Research Association (ATIRA) 67, 143
Ahmedabad Textile Millowners' Association (ATMA) **68**, **69**, 86
Ahmednagar 52
Ajay Food Stall 104
Akho 15
Al Biruni 58, **60**
Al-Faraiz-ul-Ahmadiya 55
Ali Muhammad Khan 11
Allahabad 58, 114
Al-Musililallah 55
Amdavad ni Gufa/Husain-Doshi Gufa 90, **91**, **91**
Amdavadno Itihas 11, 13
Amin, Apurva 76
Amit Ambalal 87, **88**, **89**, 90
Amod 53
Anandji Kalyanji Pedhi 13, **46**, 47, **47**
Ankleshwar 53
Anwar-i-Suhaili **40**, 41
Archer Art Gallery **84**, **85**, 91
Asarpota 67
Asarwa 26
Asma-ur Rijal 58
Astodia 117, **119**
Azad Halwai 96
Azamgarh, UP 120

B.J. Institute of Learning and Research 54
B.M. Institute of Mental Health 143
Bagh, MP 111
Bagru, Rajasthan 111, 113, 114
Baldaeus, Philip 141
Bandhej **17**, **120**, **121**, 122
Bangalore 73, 118
Bareilly 132
Batley, Claude 67, 145
Batwa 55
Bendre, N.S. 82
Bengal School 82
Benglis, Lynda 86, 87, 92
Berar, Maharashtra 52
Bhadra Fort 29
Bhagat, Niranjan 15
Bhammaria Kua, Muhammadabad 28
Bharuch 53, 107
Bhatiyar Gali **99–101**, 100
Bhatt, Jyoti 88
Bhatt, Vinod 95, 96, 105
Bhau Daji Lad Museum, Mumbai **93**
Bhavnagar 74, 81
Bhavsar, Ramnik 82
Bidar 52
Biggs, Colonel 141
Bijapur 52, 54
Bikaner 47, 132
Bohras 30, 54, 102

Briggs, H.G. 125, 128
British 10–13, 32, 33, 65, 90, 145, 148, 150
British Library **40**, 41
Brown, Percy 27
Bukhari Saiyads
    Shah Alam 53–55, 103, 131
Burgess, James 27
Burgess, Jas 11, 13, 27

(Sheth) C.N. College of Fine Arts 82, 85
Cage, John 15
Calder, Alexander 86
Calico Administrative Building 145, **147**
Calico Museum of Textiles 112, **118**
Cambay/Khambhat 10, 52, 107, 128, 143
Cartier-Bresson, Henri 107, 152
Centre for Environmental Planning and Technology (CEPT) 14, 65, 66, **72**, 74, 77, 83, 86, 90, 91
Chaghatai, M.A. 54
Champaner 54
Chandigarh 66, 145
Chandravilas restaurant 96
Chen, Long-Bin 87, 92
Chennai/Madras 13, 81
Chhaganlal Jadav Trust **16**
Chhara, Mansingh 82, **88**, 90
Chhipa, Fakruddin 122
Chhipa, Faruk 122
Chhipa, Sajid 122
Chhipas 109, 111, 117, 122
Chhipawad 117
Chhota Udaipur 114
(Sir) Chinubhai Ranccchodlal Baronet 81, 143
Chishti saints 51, 54
Chitara Govinda 41
Chitaras 122
Chitra Varga 81, 82
Chona, Satish 96
Chopra, Suneet 83
Clarke, Arthur C. 15
Community Science Centre 14
Congress party 148, 150
Contemporary Art Gallery 87–90, **88**
Correa, Charles 66, 68, 73, 75
Cunningham, Merce 15

Dada Hari Vav 28
Dadabhai Naoroji 143
Dadhichi 151
Dalits 15
Dalpatram 10, 11, 15
Damascus 55
Dang forests **112**
Dani Limda 122, **123**, 134
Dariyapur **31**, **32**
Darpana 15
Dashrath Patel Museum **108**
Daulatabad 125
Deccan Sultanates 52, 58
Deesa 112, 114
Delhi 10, 41, 47, **89**, 104, 118, 132, 134, 152
Delhi Darwaza/Idaria Darwaza 152
Delhi Sultanate 10
Desai, Ambalal Sakarlal 148
Desai, Kanu 14, 82
Devsano Pado 38
Dharampur **112**
Divali 117, 126, 129, 130
Diwan-e-Vali 62
Diwani-i-Al Aidrusi 62

Doshi, Balkrishna 66–68, **72**, 73–75, **73**, 90, 91
Dost Muhammad Shukar 54
Dube, Anita 91
Dutch 10, 141

Eames, Charles 86
East India Company 125
Egypt 52, 107
Electric House 67
Ellis Bridge/Pritam Nagar 13, 29, 33
English 10, 11, 13, 125, 141

Fakruddin Blockprinters **123**
Farrukhabad, UP 114
Fergusson, James 11, 13, 27
Festival of India exhibitions 111, **111**
Forbes, A.K. 11
Forbes, James 141

Gaekwads 11
Gajjar, Atmaram 67, 73,
Gajjar, Damodar 111, **112**, **113**, **115**, **116**
Gajjar, Maneklal 113, 114
Gamthiwala, Ahmed **114**, 122
Gandhi, Mahatma 10, 11, 14, 19, 65, 73, 81, 82, 87, 92, 105, 148, **149**, 150–52, **153**
Gandhi Smarak Sangrahalaya 73
Gandhinagar 11, 66
Ganesh Bari 29
Garhi Studio 91
Ghazali Mashhadi 52
Gillion, Kenneth 11
Girnar 36, **43**
Gomtipur 102
Government College of Fine Arts, Madras (Chennai) 81, 83
The Grand Bhagwati 104
Greens restaurant 102
Gregson, Batley and King 67
Gujarat College 13, 150
Gujarat no Tapasvi 81
Gujarat Sultanate 10, 21, 26–32, 36, 38, 39, 51, 52, 55, 144, 150
    Ahmed Shah 10, 27, 35, 51, 52, 55, 58, **59**, 150
    Mahmud Begada 10, 35, 51, 53, 55, 141
    Muzaffar Shah II 10, 51
    Zafar Khan/Muzaffar Shah I 10, 51
Gujarat University 67
Gujarat Vernacular Society 11, 143
Gujarat Vidyapith 11, 12, 81, 82
Gujarati, Devji 39, 41
Gujarati, Kesar 41
Gujarati, Meghji 41
Gujarati, Paramji 41
Gujarati, Surji 41
Gujarati, Vali 62
Gujaratnu Patnagar – Amdavad 11
Gupta, Chaman Lal 78

Hadith 53, 58, **63**
Hakim Lukman 134
Hargovandas, Amritlal 143
Harkunvar Shethani 143
Hasan Muhammad Chishti 54
Havmor 15, 96, **97**
Hazrat Abdur Rehman 54
Hazrat Pir Muhammad Shah 52, 54
Hazrat Pir Muhammad Shah (HPMS)
    Dargah Sharif Library 12, **14**, 50–63
Hemachandracharya 35

Herwitz Gallery 91
Hifz-e Maratib **55**, **62**
Hindus 19, 21, 22, 30, 38, 41, 99, 124–39, 144
Hockney, David 87
Hodgkin, Howard 86
Hope, Theodore 11, 13, 27
Husain, M.F. **90**, 91, **91**, 92,
Hutheesing Jain temple 145, **145**

Ibn Afrash 51
Ibn Khallikan 51
Indian Institute of Forest Management (IIFM), Bhopal 74
Indian Institute of Management, Ahmedabad (IIMA) 14, 66, 70, **70**, **71**, 86, 103, 143
Indian Institute of Management, Bangalore (IIMB) 73
Indian Space Research Organisation (ISRO) 66
Indore 82
Iran/Persia 11, 12, **14**, 35, 38, 41, 50–63, 55, 125, 126, 131
Irish Presbyterian Mission 13
Isanpur 114
Islam/Muslims 10, 12, 18, 19, 26, 27, 29, 30, 35, 38, 47, 51, 52, 55, 58, 102, 124–39

J.J. School of Art, Mumbai 14, 81, 82
Jadav, Chhaganlal 14, **16**, 82, **83**, 87
Jagannath *rath-yatra* **102**, 103
Jahangirnama 51
Jains 12, 18, 21, 22, 26, 29, 30, 35, 36, 37–39, 41, 43–48, 95, 99, 105, 125, 129, 131
Jaipur 39, 112, 117, 118, 120, 132
Jamalpur 85, 86, 101, 134
Jami Masjid 29, 55, 141, **144**, 145
Janmashtami 96
Jasuben Pizza 102
Jeevanlal 150
Jinadatta Suri 37, **37**
Jivandas Vadnagari 58, **60**
Jodhpur 47, 132
Joshi, Umashankar 15
Jote, Ratnamanirao 11
Jyotisangh 143

Kadamb 15
Kadi 54
Kadiya, Umakant 150
Kagdi Soniwala **126**, **130**
Kagdis 126, 129, 130, 138
Kahn, Louis 13, 66, 70, **70**, **71**, 73, 74, 86, 145
Kakani, Jaai and Surya **76**, **77**, 78
Kala Varga 81, 82
Kalpasutra/Kalakacharya Katha 35, 38, **38**
Kalupur **24**, **25**, **27**, 29
Kankaria Lake **143**, 150
Kanoria Centre for Arts 90, 91
Kanoria, Urmila 90
Kanpur 114
Kantawala, Hargovandas 148
Kanvinde, Achyut 66–68
Kapoor, Anish 87, **87**
Karachi 96
Karnatilaka 58, **60**
Karnavati 96
Kashmir 125
Kerala 104
Khadia 96, 111

154 | INDEX

Khakhar, Bhupen 85, **88**, 91
Khanpur 54
Khatri, Rashmi 82
Khimani, Yunus 91
Kinariwala, Vinod 150
Kite Museum 86, **131**, **136**
Kolkata/Calcutta 13
Kripalani, Acharya J.B. 150
Krishna, Lord **38**, 39, 58, **96**, 103, 132, 136, **139**
Krishnakumar 91
Kumar 81
Kushalchand 10
Kutch 112, 114, 117, 122
Kutiyana 53

L.D. Institute of Indology 37, 73
L.D. Museum 37, **37**, 41, **41**, 44
La Bella restaurant 102
Ladi, Prithpal Singh 91
Lahore 41, 58, 132
Lakhia, Kumudini 15
Lal Darwaza 96, 102
Lalbhai, Kasturbhai 37, 66, 143
Lalit Kala Akademi 91
Lalshankar Umiyashankar 148
Lashkari, Bechardas 148
Law Garden 104
Le Corbusier 13, 66–68, **68**, **69**, 70, 73, 74, 86, 87, 145, **146**
Lemongrasshopper Art Gallery 92, **92**
Lucknow 132
Lucknow Art College 82
Lucky restaurant 101

M.S. University, Vadodara 111
Madhavpura 114
Madhu Industries Limited 78
Madhupura Darwaza 96
Madrasa-i-Hidayat Baksh 54
Maganlal Vakhatchand 11, 13
Mahabharata 39, 58, **60**
Mahavira, Lord 48
Maidan e Shahi 29
Manav Sadhna Kendra **15**
Manek Chowk **16**, 96, **97**, **98**, 104, **104**, 114
Mangrol 53
Mansaram **88**
Mansuri, Adil 15
Marathas 10, 32, 142
Maskati & Co. **110**, 111, 112, 114
Mata Bhavani Vav 26
Mata ni Pachedi 107, 112, 120
Matar 41, **41**
Matharoo, Gurjeet Singh 74–76
Mathura 132
Maulana Ahmad bin Sulaiman Kurd 58
Maulana Muhammad bin Tahir Pattani 58, **59**
Maulana Nuruddin 54
Maulana Rumi 58
Mehta, Chunilal 148
Mehta, Keshavlal 148
Mehta, Makrand 11
Mehta, Tarak 95
Memons 102
Mies van der Rohe, Ludwig 74
The Mint 136
Minto, Lord 148
Mirat-i-Ahmadi 11, 51, 125
Miro, Joan 86
Mirza Aziz Koka 41
Mirzapur 101, 102
Mistry, C.D. **89**
Modi, Ashwin 90
Mosque of Sheikh Hasan Chishti 54
Mount Abu 36
Mughal/s 10, 12, 27, 31, 32, 35, 39, 41, 47, 52, 54, 58, 99, 102, 132, 134
   Akbar 10, 41, 47, 52, 58

Dara Shikoh **14**
Humayun **61**, 62
Jahangir 10, 41, 47, 52, 62, 141, 148
Nur Jahan 58
Shahjahan 47, 52, 58
Muharram **18**
Mumbai/Bombay 11, 13, 14, 66, 67, 81, 82, **93**, 102, 125, 131
Muni Sri Punyavijayji 37
Museum and Picture Gallery, Vadodara 41

Nagarsheth, Kushalchand 10
Nagarsheth, Sheth Shantidas Zaveri 143
Naidu, Sarojini **149**
Nair, Balkrishna 104
Nanalal Dalpatram 15, 81
Narmada river 107, 152
Nathdwara 36
National Design Collection **112**
National Institute of Design (NID) 14, 65, 66, 83, 86, **108**, **109**, 143
Navratri 117
Naziri Nishapuri 52
Neelgars 117
Newman Hall 66
Nirma University 144
Noguchi, Isamu 86
Northeast India 102, 132

Ode community 107

Padmapurana 151
Palitana 36
Pandit Baijnath 58, **60**
Pankornaka 152, **152**
Parekh, Manu 85
Parekh's store 96
Parikh, Rasiklal 82, 85
Parsis 102
Paryushan 99
Patan 10, 21, 26, 35, **36**, 37, 51, 53
   Rani ki Vav 26, 35, **36**
Patel, Balkrishna 82, **84**, 85, **85**, **88**, **89**
Patel, Bimal 74, **75**
Patel, Dashrath 83, 107, **108**, **109**
Patel, Hasmukh 66, 73
Patel, Janak **88**, 90
Patel, Jeram 14, 83, **88**
Patel, Krishna Amin **116**
Patel, Nimish 77
Patel, Pranlal **10**, **18**, 19, **143**, **146**, **147**, 148, **149**, **150**, **152**, **153**
Patel, Sardar Vallabhbhai 148, 150
Patel, Surendra 95, **131**
Pereira, Leo 67, 73, 74
Pethapur 107, 111–13, **111–13**, 115, 120, 122
Physical Research Laboratory (PRL) 15, 67, 144
Pipad, Rajasthan 114
Pir Muhammad Shah dargah 101
Piraji Sagara Art Foundation **84**, **86**
Pizza Hut 99
Portuguese 102
Pradhan, Nathu 104
Prajapatis 114
Prathama Blood Centre 74, 76
Premabhai Hall **72**, 73
Premabhai Himabhai 148
Pritam Nagar 33
Progressive Artists Group, Bombay 82
Punjab/i 52, 96, 102–04
Puratatva Mandir 11
Purohit Hotel 96

Quran 53–55, **56**, **57**, 58

Raipur Bhajiya House 96
Raipur Darwaza 96, 148

Rajasthan 41, 47, 52, 83, 107, 112–14, 117, 131, 132, 134
Raje, Anant 66, 73
Rajvinod 51
Raksha Bandhan 134
Ramayana 39, 150
Rampur 132
Ramzan 103, **103**
Ranakpur 36
Ranchhodlal Chhotalal 11, **142**, **143**, 148
Rangrezes
   Feroze **119**
   Hanif 117, **119**
   Khatum Bibi **119**
Rani no Hajiro 114
Rasulabad 53
Rauschenberg, Robert 87, 92
Raval, Ravishankar 14, 81–83
Rawal, Trupti 11
Reddy, Ravinder 91
Relia, Anil **84**, **85**, 91
Relief Road 101
Rewal, Raj 75
Rimzon, N.N. 91
Roe, Sir Thomas 148
Rosenquist, James 86
Roy Chowdhury, Deviprasad 83

Sa'di 62
Sabarmati Ashram 105
Sabarmati river **6**, 10, 18, 53, 65, 73, 96, 106–23, **150**, 151
Sabarmati Riverfront Development Project 74, 76
Sagaras
   Ishwar 86, **86**
   Piraji 14, 82, 83, **84**, 85, 86, **86**, **89**, 90
   Rajesh **6**, 92, **92**
Sahasralinga Talao 26
Samvegi Jain Upashraya **43**, 44
Sanganer, Rajasthan 113, 114
Sangath **6**, 66, 73, **73**
Sankalp Hotel 96
Sanskar Kendra 70
Santiniketan 81, 82
Saptak Music Festival 15
Sarabhai Foundation 86, 87
Sarabhai House 70, 87, **87**, 92
Sarabhais
   Ambalal 66, 81, 143
   Gautam 66
   Gira 66
   Mrinalini 15
   Mrudula 150
   Sarlaben 81
   Vikram 14, 66, 143
Sarasvati river 26
Sarkhej 35, 53, 103, 109
School of Architecture *see* CEPT
Sen Kapadia 66
Shah, Archana **17**, 120, **120**, **121**, 122
Shah, Bhanu 82, 86, 90, **136**
Shah, Gajendra 82
Shah, Haku 82
Shah, Himmat 85
Shah, Sharad 66
Shah, Wajihuddin Alawi **53**, 54
Shahibag 54
Shahpur 54, 120
Shaikh Abdul-Latif Abbasi 58
Shams Khan Masjid 54
Sharfuddin Yazdi 41
Sharhah Shatibi 58, **59**
Shatrunjaya 36, 43, **43**, 44, **47**
Sheikh Ahmed Khattu 35, 52, 53, **52**, 55, 103
Sheikh, Gulammohammed 85
Sheikh Uthman 53
Sheth, Shantidas 47
Shetty, Sudarshan 92, **93**

Shodhan House 70
Sidi Saiyyad mosque 92, 141, **142**, **150**
Sindh 96, 102, 104
Singh, Martand 111
Solankis 21, 22, 26
   Jaisimha Siddharaj 35
   Kumarapal 35, 99
Somani, Narendra 104
Sonnier, Keith 86
Space Application Centre (SAC) 142, 143
Stella, Frank 86, 87
Stock Exchange (old) 96
Sufism 38, 52, 54, 55, **55**, 131
   Qadiri Shattaris 54
Suhrawardy saints
   Burhanuddin Qutb-i-Alam 55
   Syed Jalaluddin 62
Sundaram 15
Surat 47, **49**, 53, 74, 107, 111, 112, 114, 125
Swadeshi Udyovardhak Mandali 148
Swadeshi Vastu Sahakar Mandali 148
Swaminarayans 36, 99
Swaminathan, J. 83

Tagore, Rabindranath 11, 81
Tankshal 135
Thailand/Siam 102, 107, **110**, 111–13
Thakardas 117
Thaker, Labhshanker 95, 105
Thakores 114
Thalmann, Gerard 87
Torrent Pharmaceuticals 77
Town Hall 15, 67, **146**
Triennale 1973 86
Tughra 54
Turner, J.M.W. 82

Udaivilas Palace, Udaipur 78
UNESCO World Heritage Site 19
United Bengal Home **148**
Usha Theatre 101
Utran/Makar Sankranti 131, **131**, 132, 134, 136, 138, **139**
Uttar Pradesh 114, 120, 132, 134

V.S. Hospital **149**
Vadigam 96
Vadodara/Baroda 41, 85, 87, 92, 111, **113**
Vagharis 120
Vaghela, Karan 26
Vaishnavas 18, 36, 39, 99, 136, **139**
Vakhatchand, Maganlal 11, 13
Vallabhis 35
Vasna 96, 107, 120
Vastrapur 104
Vidyadevi Patli 37
Vishala 95, **105**
Vishwakarma Collection 111
Visual Art Centre/Hutheesing Art Centre 90
Vividha-tirtha-pata **43**, 44, **46**

Wowo 90
Wright, Frank Lloyd 66, 145, **147**

Yagnik, Indulal 150
Yaqoot al Mustasami 62
Yasin Savaijiwala **110**, 114
Yusuf bin Ahmed bin Muhammad bin Uthman 51, 53

Zaveri, Parul 77, 78

Contributors

Suchitra Balasubrahmanyan studied visual communication at the National Institute of Design and teaches at the Faculty of Arts and Humanities, CEPT University. Her research and teaching interests include design history, orality and visual literacy, and the sociology of design. She is co-author of *The Shaping of Modern Gujarat: Plurality, Hindutva and Beyond* (2005) and *Ahmedabad: From Royal City to Megacity* (2011).

Sharmila Sagara studied sculpture at the Faculty of Fine Arts, M.S. University, Baroda and has participated in group shows, curated exhibitions, and written in newspapers and art journals as an art critic. She headed the Kanoria Centre for Arts (2001–05) and is presently Associate Professor at the Faculty of Arts and Humanities, CEPT University.

R.J. Vasavada is Professor and Head of the post-graduate programme in Architectural and Settlement Conservation at CEPT University. He was Assistant Architect to Professor Louis Kahn for the IIM, Ahmedabad project. His areas of interest include the history of architecture, temple architecture, stepwells, and the social culture of towns in the historic context especially related to heritage conservation and restoration.

Shridhar Andhare was Director of the Lalbhai Dalpatbhai Museum and Honorary Director of the N.C. Mehta Gallery, Ahmedabad. He specializes in the history of miniature painting of Rajasthan and western India. He is the author of *Chronology of Mewar Painting* (1987), the Devgadh and Bundi portfolios of Lalit Kala Akademi, and the L.D. Museum catalogue.

Mohaiuddin Bombaywala taught Persian and Urdu at various colleges before retiring as Professor of Urdu at Gujarat Vidyapith. He has been director of the Hazrat Pir Muhammad Shah Dargah Sharif Library since 1998 and edited the library's 10-volume catalogue. He has received the President's Award for Lifetime Achievement in Urdu and Persian and the Gujarat government's Gaurav Puraskar.

Himanshu Burte, architect and writer, teaches at the School of Habitat Studies, Tata Institute of Social Sciences, Mumbai. His first book, *Space for Engagement: The Indian Artplace and a Habitational Approach to Architecture* (2008) won critical acclaim in India and abroad. He was a Fulbright Fellow at the University of California, Berkeley, and Project for Public Spaces, New York in 2008–09.

Sheela Bhatt is a senior journalist based in New Delhi. She was founder editor of the Gujarati weekly *Abhiyan* and senior editor of the Gujarati edition of *India Today*. At present she is editorial director of www.rediff.com. She received the Chameli Devi Jain Award for Outstanding Woman Mediaperson in 1993.

Aditi Ranjan is a weaver, textile designer, and design teacher at the National Institute of Design. She was a consultant at the Indus Valley School of Art and Design, Karachi and visiting faculty at National College of Art, Craft and Design, Stockholm. She has worked with the handloom and handicrafts sector, conducted international seminars on *bandhani*, and is author of *Textile and Bamboo Crafts of Northeast India* (1983) and co-editor of *Handmade in India* (2007).

Yatin Pandya is an author, activist, academician, researcher, as well as practising architect, with his firm FOOTPRINTS E.A.R.T.H. (Environment Architecture Research Technology Housing). He has been involved with city planning, urban design, mass housing, architecture, interior design, product design, and conservation projects. His publications include *Concepts of Space in Traditional Indian Architecture* and *Elements of Space Making*. He has won awards for architectural design and research.